The Miracle of Optimism

Kevin M. Touhey (signature)

Change Your Perspective, Change Your Life

KEVIN M. TOUHEY

Published by
Archer Ellison Publishing, Inc.
P.O. Box 950696
Lake Mary, FL 32795

Visit
TheMiracleOfOptimism.com
GiftOfOptimism.com
TheMiracleOfOptimismSystem

Library of Congress Control Number: 2009909616
ISBN 13: 978-1-57472-377-9

CONTENTS

PART 3: CONSISTENCY

PART 4: APPRECIATION

PART 5: PERSONAL GROWTH

DEDICATION

MY SIBLINGS

Kathleen, Maureen, Eileen, Brian, Dennis,
Regina (with God), Timothy, Patrick, Michael

THE CINDERELLA FAMILY

"Souls bound in sorrow will never be broken...they wait
for each other to catch up...peace will always be ours
whenever we're together because these ties were born out of
such sorrows and have a silent respect and love for one another.
I believe the calm comes from that common thread."
—My brother J. Brian Touhey

The following is an email from my brother
Brian to me while I was writing this book:

"Through all of our troubled times I was bound to all of my brothers and sisters. Whenever I saw any of you suffering I felt it too...the
hunger...the beatings...the humiliations...and I am sure in the deepest part of my soul, I know they all felt for me too...out of that tremendous dysfunction a bond of love was born, that no matter what
became of any us we would always have that love...early on we sometimes loved each other in an unhealthy manner, but nonetheless we
tried...just as we tried to make every bad situation in our childhoods
better...now we have taken that bond to another level I believe...we
all see the tremendous pain we all suffered and now see it in a different light...one that shows us that love and forgiveness can heal any
scar whether it was mental, emotional, or spiritual... these gifts are

truly boundless...God has opened each of our hearts to this truth at different times...this is why there is this calm between all of us that says, no matter what we will all be OK...in my soul I know we all will know true peace and I know that our father and sister are working on that for all of us...what a beautiful gift God has given us...the ability to survive the insanity and put our lives back together and then to know that it is so true that out of pain is born a unique ability to love in a deeper way then one could ever have imagined...Love, Bri"

MY SIBLINGS, MY HEROES

I went to see the movie *Cinderella Man* with my mom while I was in the process of writing this book. The movie is about the fortitude and struggles of heavyweight boxer James J. Braddock to earn enough money to feed his family.

There is a scene in the movie in which they have no heat and the children are very cold. Braddock's wife and children resort to tearing a fence apart so they can burn the wood to stay warm. My family, too, had to resort to that when we had no coal for the furnace. The scene brought tears to my eyes, but not because it reminded me of my brothers and me prying pieces of wood out of the basement of the abandoned house next door so we could stay warm. I cried because I could feel the pride of the Braddock family and their determination to overcome their seemingly insurmountable financial circumstances. I could feel their embarrassment over their situation since it was so familiar to me.

While I was watching that scene about the Braddock family, I connected with the absolute resourcefulness we needed in my own family because we did not have enough of anything. I felt the spirit of my siblings in that scene: my sisters, Kathleen, Maureen, Eileen, and Regina, and my brothers, Brian, Dennis, Timothy, Patrick, and Michael. I felt their hope and faith that the bright light hand of help was going to emerge out of this darkness called poverty to pull us from its grasp. The pure love I felt for all of my siblings in that moment made me cry. Watching that scene in the movie made me respect the deep souls of my siblings more than ever before.

The fact that James J. Braddock overcame incredible odds to win the heavyweight championship over the seemingly unbeatable Max Baer reminded me how every one of my siblings struggled and triumphed over seemingly insurmountable odds to become the champions they are today.

With love,
Kevin M. Touhey

FOREWORD

It was Helen Keller who said: *Life is either a daring adventure or nothing. To keep our faces toward change and behave like free spirits in the presence of fate is strength undefeatable.*

I recommend that you dare to venture inside this book: *The Miracle of Optimism*. Kevin has brilliantly arranged the flow and format of this book as he shares his remarkable story, providing you with pearls of wisdom and allowing you to experience and learn from his journey and your own. There isn't another book like this on the market today, nor do I believe there will ever be another one like it.

What I enjoyed most about *The Miracle of Optimism* is that Kevin gives you the opportunity to experience and increase your own level of optimism. Optimism can be the fuel to skyrocket your dreams to new heights. Conversely, optimism often gets blocked when we refuse to let go of the painful emotions from the past. Inside the pages of this treasure you will uncover the miracles that occur when you simply "let go" and reconnect to your own passion. You have the choice right now to take the first step and commit to all of the powerful exercises Kevin has created for you.

There is a story in this book in which Kevin talks about "losing his voice" and the consequences he experienced from doing so. I cringed when I read this story and you may too, but I know Kevin shares this story from a place of love. You will find that many of Kevin's own stories, anecdotes, and recommendations will stay with you for a long time after you have read this book. So many people "lose their voices" and are blindsided by the hurtful outcomes. When you follow all of the exercises outlined in this book, the journey becomes your own. You can choose to reflect, forgive, learn, and heal from your past pains—or you can choose to keep holding on to them with the false illusion that they are your life preserver, when in actuality they are cement blocks weighing you down.

The emotional release you will experience from *The Miracle of Optimism* can be the equivalent to cutting the sandbags that keep the hotair balloon secured to the ground. Emotions can get the better of you or they can help you soar to new heights. Kevin will show you how to soar.

Many years ago I received a card from Successories. This card became a "reminder card" for me that I kept in front of me at all times. This is what it said:

The Essence of a New Day
Author Unknown
This is the beginning of a new day. You have been given this day to use as you will. You can waste it or use it for good. What you do today is important because you are exchanging a day of your life for it. When tomorrow comes, this day will be gone forever; in its place is something that you have left behind...let it be something good.

You have a tremendous opportunity in front of you right now. Today is your chance to decide to go on this journey with Kevin. Allow him to take you deep within and perhaps voyage through your own painful past. Forgive, heal, and begin to create a new life—a life renewed and filled with optimism.

Peggy McColl
New York Times best-selling author, *Your Destiny Switch*

PREFACE

"THERE ARE A LOT OF PEOPLE STRIVING
BUT VERY FEW ARRIVING."
> —*Wayne Dyer*

"Mr. Touhey," said the paramedics as I lay on the floor in the refreshment concourse of the new Lincoln Financial Stadium in Philadelphia. "You're in trouble here." The year was 2003.

I looked up at my brother Tim. "Take care of the kids," I said.

"I have them covered," Tim said. "Just pay attention to the medics!"

"That's not what I mean," I thought, but couldn't speak the words. Blood was streaming from my nose and mouth, and the medics were racing to stop the bleeding. What I really meant was, "If I die right now, will you take care of the kids?"

As the paramedics worked on me my mind began to drift. Have I told Annabelle enough times that she is the love of my life? Have I fought so hard over the last two years only to die now? My daughters, Serena, just three years old, and Ava, only a few months old—will I never again enjoy the wonder of my children?

The commotion around me continued as I mourned my life. If I died now, I would not get to sing my song here on earth. I had not contributed everything I wanted to contribute. I could not accept this as the end.

While I was contemplating giving up, the paramedics had not; quickly and professionally, they were doing everything possible to save my life. My blood pressure was so high that they did not know whether to give me nitroglycerin to prevent a heart attack or try to stop the bleeding first. If they gave me the nitro first, they might not be able to stop the hemorrhaging. If they tried to stop the bleeding first, I might have a stroke or a heart attack. They were in a difficult situation.

But just as events seemed to be at their worst, I felt a familiar presence; something warm, wonderful, and utterly miraculous, a presence that is stronger than death. This presence had saved me many times before and now I felt it again. I even heard it, this small, soft voice, speaking from within, tugging me gently out of death's clutches.

"Kevin," the voice said,"you have to make it through this.You're not finished here!"

Meanwhile the paramedics decided to give me an intravenous drug that would stop the bleeding first; then they immediately put a nitro strip under my tongue. It worked.My blood pressure, which had been 220 over 160, began to drop and the bleeding stopped.

The presence remained with me as I began to stabilize. "And once you do get through this," I heard, "you must stop struggling with life. Life is not a game to be won but a gift to be enjoyed. Your happiness does not depend on success!"

As the paramedics put me on to the gurney for the trip to the hospital, I began to finally see that life depends on just the *opposite* of what most people define as success. Success to me would forever have a new meaning: acknowledging the gifts and blessings that are all around me. I need to allow these gifts to uplift my spirit; to simply relax and receive all good things into my life because it is my birthright; to enjoy each and every moment as if it is my last.

I wasn't "out of the woods" yet. These revelations took a while to sink in. Once I was in the emergency room, I was still extremely upset and scared, until one of the many gifts in my life, my mother-in-law, arrived. Beside the fact that she is a doctor and I really trust her, she exudes a sense of motherly comfort wherever she goes, and I needed that now. It wasn't until her arrival that I felt I could start to calm down.

I spent five days in the hospital: a lot of time to think, reflect, and be grateful. I began to realize I had invited some conditions and circumstances into my life that were crushing my spirit. I was facing financial collapse. I was working day and night to keep the creditors at bay because a few investors in my company had made some financial decisions without my knowledge that nearly put me out of business. I struggled for nearly two years under tremendous pressure to save my business. Finally, my body just gave in and stopped me in my tracks.

My life changed that day at the Temple–Rutgers game at the Linc. It was then that I realized that all the answers were within me—that the joy I was searching for was a matter of changing the way I perceived the circumstances and conditions of my life. That included looking at my childhood from a different point of view—not through rose-colored glasses, but from a connection with the deep spirit of my soul. Forgiving myself and all others would be the key to unlock the unprecedented peace and joy that I desired in my life.

I had been searching in all the wrong places and waiting for some new circumstance in my life or in the outside world to bring the change. These changes needed to be made in my soul. This *knowing* came from remembering my birthright: to live a life full of miracles, joy, and optimism. I just needed to use the tools of my spirit to change.

Whether there was any real chance I would die that day is irrelevant. The change in my perception led me down the path of believing that everything in my world is okay. I want for nothing, I long for nothing, and I have everything I need right here, right now, inside my soul. I still have some rough times in my life despite this incident and the profound changes in the way I think and feel. The difference is that now I am better able to put my problems in a more positive perspective. I can see them now for what they are—little bumps in the road.

PART

1

THE
FOUNDATIONS
OF OPTIMISM

1
Beginning the Journey

> "I BELIEVE THAT WE ARE HERE TO
> CONTRIBUTE LOVE TO THE PLANET—EACH
> OF US IN OUR OWN WAY."
> — *Bernie Siegel*

THE PURPOSE OF THIS BOOK

I've written this book because one of the core values I live by is contributing to others. I've been told countless times that the stories of my life are very compelling and should be shared. If this story inspires others, the purpose of the book is realized.

GREATER SELF-AWARENESS

My main goal in this book is to guide you on a journey to self-awareness, personally, professionally, and spiritually, by sharing my journey. Self-awareness helped me eliminate an incredible amount of negativity and furthered my commitment to contribute to others. By eliminating negative thoughts and feeling states, I have been able to access the spirit of optimism that resides inside of me. Self-awareness has become the key to awakening my soul. Self-awareness has helped me recognize my profound birthright of being a caring, loving, knowing, believing, and optimistic beacon of light.

This book is an expression of that awareness. It has taken a lifetime of experiences and a short time of intentional self-awareness to piece together the way my foundation of hope withstood the some-times very harsh experiences of my life. I've evolved into believing that I can have a life free from the madness of my inner thoughts and emotions. I now have a firm belief that everything in my wonderful life is magnificent.

MANAGING YOUR OWN LIFE STRUGGLES USING THE FIVE "FEELING STATES"

Another purpose of this book is to help you discover the path toward managing your own life struggles. Although it may seem simplistic, the book's message can be helpful to anyone who finds himself or herself in one of the following five categories, which I call feeling states:

1. The **"borderline of joy"** state. You feel that you are on the verge of great things in your life. You're just seeking the key that will open the door to fantastic, enthusiastic living.
2. The **"so-so"** state. You live a relatively happy life, but lack real passion and exuberance.
3. The **"apathetic"** state. You are living in a comfortable level of pain— you're unhappy but you accept it as "just life."
4. The **"barely functioning"** state. You are in a world of pain, con-tinuing to get by, but just barely. You live life as if it is something to be endured, lacking any real happiness or joy.
5. The **"shut down"** state. The wear and tear of your life's problems has just worn you out. You may be addicted to alcohol, drugs, sex, or work, or you may even be suicidal.

I know well these states of being—because I have lived portions of my life in each. I have empathy for those I encounter who are stuck in any of these phases, as each can be very painful. During my journey through these phases, I became a little more functional, only to discover that once I got *the job,* or *this relationship,* or *this amount of money,* I felt some level of relief or even some happiness. However, I discovered there would be no feeling of real, lasting, sustainable joy.

The stories, lessons, exercises, and tools here are designed to manifest good for all who embark on the book's journey. It is your journey, too.

CREATING AND MANIFESTING A REWARDING AND FULFILLING LIFE

"THERE ARE ONLY TWO WAYS TO LIVE
YOUR LIFE. ONE IS AS THOUGH NOTHING
IS A MIRACLE. THE OTHER IS AS THOUGH
EVERYTHING IS A MIRACLE."
—*Albert Einstein*

The ultimate purpose of this book is to help you change your life to fulfill your dreams and make it the life you want to live. My goal is to help you push aside those obstacles that are keeping you from having a life filled with miracles. You'll do this by reading and working through the lessons.

Miracles can occur every day when we live with self-awareness. When we are in touch with our thoughts, feelings, and emotions, it is easy to see the flood of miracles that are present in our lives. When you start to recognize the miracles, then you can begin to live each and every day with unbridled energy in a feeling state called optimism.

My own evolution from *hoping* to *believing* to *knowing* is the basis of this book. The energy, power, and peace that I feel in my life today are what allow the words to flow from my soul, my deepest spirit. So many circumstances in my life demonstrated that I just needed to remember that the source of all power in my life resides right inside me. This is true of everyone; the source and power of healing and optimistic living reside within you, too. I know this book can be an inspiration to those who turn its pages. I know we live in a wonderful world created for our good. I know that my mother and father loved me on the deepest level that parents can love a child. I know that the soul of God, my soul, and the soul of my parents are one. I know that my life is a Miracle of Optimism. I know my life is perfect...with a thousand interruptions!

A WORD OF CAUTION

As you read my life story, you may think that your life circumstances were never as extreme as mine, so the book will not have anything to say to you. Or perhaps your life experiences were much worse, so the message and purpose of this book will not hold true for you.

During the past ten years in my coaching practice, I have worked with teens and adults in a wide range of circumstances. I've worked with people who have endured every type of abuse, highly successful executives who are grinding their way through unfulfilled lives, and every type of life in between. The message, lessons, exercises, and healing tools in this book will work for anyone, no matter what your background or life circumstances. I have used these tools across the spectrum of human experience, from the least functional people to highly functional, financially successful people with seemingly perfect lives who remain extremely unhappy.

ARE YOU READY TO BEGIN?

For the next two hundred or so pages, I invite you to join me on this road of life with all its little bumps and potholes and obstacles along the way. As we walk together, I will share some of my stories with you, primarily from the first twenty-one years of my life. Before we begin, I suggest that you find a walking stick (for our purposes, a pencil or pen will do just fine) and a pad of paper to write your own stories as I tell mine. Then share your stories with someone close to you. No matter how you use this book, thank you for sharing this journey with me!

HOW TO READ THIS BOOK

There are four basic human needs for a healthy life. Different sections of the book will address each of these needs. I share stories of my own life as it relates to these four tenets of human development. Consequently, the stories and anecdotes are not chronological but topical as they relate to the four basic tenets.

Who or what is holding you back? Your boss? Your career? In my coaching practice, the answer I hear most often is "My family of origin." This is also the answer I used a lot in my life when things were not going my way.

A healthy family environment comprises four essential elements:

1. Each member is appreciated for who he or she is.
2. There is consistency in relationships and interactions among family members (especially true early in life with children and caretakers).
3. Each member feels like he belongs to something—a family, a community, something larger than himself. Each feels a measure of inclusion.
4. Each person experiences a measure of positive personal growth in all her human interactions, something that moves her in the direction she wants her life to take.

All children and adults need these four essential elements as they move through their life experiences to be healthy, happy human spirits.

What exactly is a "healthy family"? I use a scale of 1 to 10 to describe how we perceive the circumstances of our upbringing. A score of 10 indicates highly functional and healthy; 1 is low-functioning and unhealthy. Every family scenario is somewhere on this scale. When our family situation is low on the scale and we don't get these four essential elements while growing up, we default to some behavior to fill the void. This may include adopting unhealthy attitudes and perceptions. I know that in my own life I have defaulted to overwork, overeating, excessive drinking, and other unhealthy behaviors. With a measure of self-awareness, we can develop our own system for receiving the four essential elements.

Consider your own family background. Where on the scale would you place your family experience? You should consider that your score for each of the categories may be different. Understanding this concept will assist you in tracing where the blocks were erected to impede your life, a life that could be overflowing with miracles, joy, and optimism.

For example, in my own family life I scored high on item #3. I felt I was part of the Touhey family, part of the sports teams I played on, and in other ways part of a larger whole. But the scores on the other elements weren't so high. I didn't always feel appreciated for the unique qualities of my personality, and there was not much consistency in my childhood.

DEFINITION OF TERMS

There are several terms I refer to whose common meaning you understand, but I may be using them to mean something different from what you expect.

Hope: I define hope as having the faith that no matter how bad the conditions or circumstances at the moment, good things are right around the corner if we just hang in there. You'll see this term often as we go on.

Optimism: Optimism is the sibling of hope. When I call myself an optimist, I assure you I am not 100 percent happy and smiling all the time. I still have challenging days. But when you live life with an optimist's outlook, those rough spots seem so much smoother!

Miracles: The dictionary defines "miracle" as "an effect or extraordinary event in the physical world that surpasses all known human or natural powers and is ascribed to a supernatural cause; such an effect or event manifesting or considered as a work of God." When you think of miracles, perhaps you are envisioning miraculous healings or other dramatic events. When I use the word "miracle," I am suggesting that miracles are all around us and touch us every day. In fact, sometimes miracles are hidden within the darkest moments of our lives. That's where they have often manifested in my life.

The ego: The blocks to optimism are erected in the ego. In this book, when I refer to the ego, I am decribing three elements that work hard to keep you from positive personal growth. The ego will:

- Want to make you right about everything
- Want you to justify all your thoughts, feelings, and behaviors
- Want you to dominate and control all situations

I urge you to read the lessons and do the exercises throughout the book. They will help you figure out where you acquired the perceptions, behaviors, and attitudes that are holding you back. Some of the exercises will ask you to go back in time to look at the past; some take place in real time. I have conducted these exercises with thousands of people. They work, so do them diligently. This book is not just a story about me, but a wonderful story of how you can change your own life!

As you read the book and do the exercises, keep the four essential elements of healthy development in mind. This will make the exercises more powerful.

THE IMPORTANCE OF HOPE: THE FOUNDATION FOR OPTIMISM

"WE MUST ACCEPT FINITE DISAPPOINTMENT,
BUT NEVER LOSE INFINITE HOPE."
— *Martin Luther King Jr.*

As noted above, I define hope as having the faith that no matter how bad the conditions or circumstances of life at the moment, good things are right around the corner if we just hang in there. My foundation for holding onto hope was profound and deep-rooted, even mystical. But hope is also a skill I have developed and nurtured.

HOW PERCEPTION AFFECTS OUR BELIEFS

"EVERY SECOND IS A DOOR TO ETERNITY.
THE DOOR IS OPENED BY PERCEPTION."
— *Rumi*

The key to any person's development is his perception of circumstances and his belief system. As I describe in the following chapters, my belief system wavered back and forth. Some beliefs that I adopted were not healthy. I defaulted to them because I did not have those four essential elements for healthy development that children need to form a solid foundation. If these important ingredients are lacking, the result may be an inability to experience personal growth. So I continued to recreate experiences and situations that recalled my childhood experiences of feeling unappreciated, not appreciating others, and living in very inconsistent conditions. I manifested the career of college coaching to recreate that feeling of belonging that was high on the scale for me.

Even when my belief system was so out of whack that all I felt was pain, I still held on to hope. I knew I had to keep searching because buried within was the hope that there had to be more to life than I was experiencing. Many people asked me, "What more do you want?"I was labeled "restless" and not grateful enough for the career I had. Though I continued living the so-called perfect life, I was dealing with a lot of inner turmoil. I kept up appearances, but I could not deny my yearning to keep searching, to hang on to hope that I would find my way to greater joy.

WHY STORIES ARE IMPORTANT

As you continue to read the stories in this book, you will find that I'm a first-generation Irishman. The Irish are known not only for St. Patrick's Day, but for their storytelling. This book will tell a lot of stories. But you don't need to be Irish to tell a story about yourself. Anyone who was ever born has a story to tell. So as you read my stories, think about events in your own life. After each lesson and exercise , you will have space to write your own journal.

PEARLS

Watch for these words of wisdom placed throughout the book to highlight certain aspects of the lessons being given.

> *"A pearl is a beautiful thing that is produced by an injured life. It is the tear [that results] from the injury of the oyster. The treasure of our being in this world is also produced by an injured life. If we had not been wounded, if we had not been injured, then we will not produce the pearl."* —S. Heller

LESSON 1

SELF-AWARENESS: THE KEY TO AWAKENING THE SOUL

> "WHEN I DISCOVER WHO I AM, I'LL BE FREE."
>
> — *Ralph Ellison*

To truly move forward and live the life of your dreams takes a measure of awareness. I sometimes think people are sleepwalking through life. They aren't alert to the present moment.

> *Look Within: Self-awareness is the key to awakening the soul. The kind of self-awareness needed to take responsibility for your own power and growth is rare today. Most people look outside themselves for someone to blame or for someone else to provide the answers.*

I once attended a workshop facilitated by Dave Ellis called Falling Awake. He urged us to pay attention to what was going on in our lives. John Lennon sang, "Life is what happens to you while you're busy making other plans." Most people believe that almost everything that happens in their lives is out of their control. But the circumstances and situations in your life have been invited to your life's party—and you're the one who invited them. This lesson's exercise is to help you get in touch with some of the feelings or thoughts you may not be consciously aware of.

> *Take Responsibility: Becoming aware of your thoughts, feelings, and actions will help you take responsibility for any negative energy responses and then change them.*

As you will see from my stories in later chapters, I made major decisions in my life by disregarding what my intuition was trying to tell me. I denied myself access to the awareness that resided inside of me. Sometimes those intuitions were screaming at me loudly, only to be ignored by my ego.

The first step in taking responsibility is to conduct a diligent self-evaluation and to become acutely aware of how you perceive life. These exercises will be the starting point for revealing how you are spending your energy in the present. It takes energy to live life to the fullest. If you are expending more negative energy than gaining positive, it will be difficult to sustain a life full of joy and happiness.

> *Become the Observer: Self-awareness is the capacity to stand apart from ourselves and examine our behavior, intentions, thoughts, and feelings about what is happening around us.*

Note: If done diligently, this exercise will help you start to uncover your blocks to optimism. Some of your beliefs about your limitations will also come to the forefront. It takes energy to be optimistic, and making excuses drains your energy.

After each lesson and exercise in the book, you will have space to write your own journal. Write a few sentences about how the information in the chapter preceding each lesson and exercise relates to your life.

Exercise 1

THE FEELING STATES

Please take a few minutes and journal in the space provided. Review the feeling states from page 8 carefully. Be honest with yourself as you either choose the state that you are in or combine a few to describe yourself. If you are feeling a certain way and none of the feeling states seems to fit, describe that feeling state in your own words.

Please give some examples from your life that support your self-evaluation. If you are living in the "borderline of joy" state, give some real-life examples of how you could have opened the door to fantastic living. Be specific and precise in your answers. Self-awareness requires diligence. Have fun and good luck!

_____

_____

_____

_____

_____

_____

_____

_____

2

The Miracle of Hope

"HOPE CAN HAVE NO BASE EXCEPT IN FAITH."
— *Erich Fromm*

It's a boy!!! When my mother went into labor with me, my father walked out of St. Mary's Hospital in Passaic, New Jersey, knelt on a stone kneeler, and prayed for six hours. Hope is considered one of the three main Christian virtues, and my father, who was Roman Catholic (Irish Catholic and proud of it), held tightly to hope as he prayed during my mother's labor. It was this prayer vigil that began my life journey marked by hope—hope that would stand against all obstacles that lay ahead.

I believe that all souls are connected, and so my soul and my father's soul are one. Therefore, the prayers of hope he offered throughout my mother's pregnancy took root within my soul. I received those prayers, and the first seeds of hope were planted before my entrance into the physical world.

After my three older sisters, Kathleen, Maureen, and Eileen, were born into the Touhey family, my father prayed for a son and really believed that his next child would be a son. A son could be taught to play ball, follow in his footsteps as a police officer, and go with him to the firing range and football games. Finally, Jim Touhey would be able to love and raise a son in the way he wished his father had raised him. His heart was full of hope, optimism, and limitless possibilities.

I believe that this connection of hope and love that I had with my father had an effect on me even before birth, on a spiritual and even a cellular level. I probably could not wait to come into this world so full of love and happiness. Without knowing it, my father had bestowed a gift upon me that I would use for a lifetime. Even when life threw its worst at me, when my sense of hope was most challenged, I always believed that my circumstances could change if I just hung on a little longer.

In the book *Feelings Buried Alive Never Die,* Karol K. Truman writes that many of our feelings and some of our beliefs are established before we are born: "We are sensitive to the feelings our parents were experiencing during our gestation period." In that book he cites research from *The Secret Life of the Unborn Child,* by Thomas Verny, MD. Dr. Verny says, "We now know that the unborn child is an aware, reacting human being who from the sixth month on leads an active emotional life." Truman continues, "What the child experiences in the womb creates predispositions, expectations, and vulnerabilities."

I was predisposed to the feeling of hope because of my father's attitude about the possibilities of having a son. He exhibited an attitude of excitement and hope for my birth all during my mother's pregnancy. My mother also wanted my father to have a son. She had feelings of hope and possibility, too. Thank God I was a boy. Really!

I was a healthy ten-pound baby boy. My mom tells me I was a very happy baby, full of life and ready to face the world each day with enthusiasm. She said I was potty trained at the age of one year. I just didn't want to be encumbered with these things called diapers!

The early years of my life were spent in a post–World War II army barracks converted for returning veterans. Our house had four rooms: two bedrooms, a living room, and a kitchen. My parents had one bedroom and I shared the other with my sisters. When I was three my brother Brian was born. Now there were five children sharing one bedroom! Our house was no palace, but it was full of love and joy and hope.

I know my sisters loved me very dearly. They took care of me and included me in their play, often in the woods up the hill behind our house. I marveled at their ability to climb the trees. I remember them taking me up that hill, carrying cardboard boxes for sleds, and sliding down the hill laughing gleefully. My sister Eileen took me for walks after she got home from kindergarten. She tells me I loved walking through all the laundry in the back yards of the homes in the barracks. My heart soaked up their love like a sponge, and my prayer-given sense of hope grew stronger by the day.

I loved my father and was very proud that he was a police officer. I loved seeing him in his uniform and knowing that I could feel safe because he would protect us from the bad guys. He took me to the firing range and I watched as he practiced his shooting. Once, he took me to the jail so I could see where the bad guys lived. I even got to ride in his police car, and that made me feel really special. I was his "right-hand man." I know that my father loved me very much.

One day a kid who lived in the barracks bet me that I couldn't drink the kerosene that was used to heat the homes. Not one to turn down a bet, I rose to the challenge and downed some of the noxious fuel. After my sisters rushed me home, my father gave me a glass of milk and called in his buddies on the police force to rush me to the hospital. Another time, I had a recurring dream that a black cat was attacking me. I woke up and screamed for my father. He hurried to my bedside to soothe me, then took me to his bed and snuggled me close to keep that cat away. My love for him knew no bounds.

As a young child, I truly believed that all was okay in the Touhey household. I felt loved, nurtured, included, and appreciated. But as I grew older, I began to see that all was not okay. In many ways my father was very protective of us—but he was not always able to protect us from himself.

> *Self-esteem is a core, heartfelt feeling of worthiness; self-confidence is a mind exercise that is more susceptible to change, based upon condition.*

SPORTS: A NEW BASIS FOR HOPE EMERGES

I began to love sports at a young age. Sports would provide one of the key elements that every child needs: to be included.

My father introduced me to sports and was my first hero. I remember one very cold Thanksgiving Day when he took me and two older cousins, Joe and Rob, to see the Nutley-Kearny football game.

It was heaven being with these guys. We stood in the end zone behind the fence and watched the game. It was cold and my dad and cousins took me to the men's room periodically to be sure I didn't freeze. I felt so cared about, so appreciated for being the little boy that I was, and mostly I felt like I belonged to a strong family unit. In those moments, I really believed I was the answer to my dad's hopes of having a son. The joy my father showed on these outings made a deep impression on me; it just felt right. The man who showed such joy, caring, and love was my real father.

The joy of sport became a powerful emotional memory for me. Sporting events allowed me to feel included, appreciated, and safe. But like everything else in a family as dysfunctional as mine, the experience of sports would soon lose its innocence and joy. I was the child for whom my father knelt on a stone kneeler for six hours, pleading his case for a boy. The fact that his prayer was answered put a lot of pressure on me to be special, right from the beginning.

At first I didn't feel that pressure. I was my dad's right-hand man. I could not wait to get home from school so I could go with him to the park to coach my cousins and the rest of the neighborhood team. My dad coached my cousins Joe and Rob in a football league that was less formal than the official Pop Warner teams, but still competitive. I used to love going down to the field after dinner for practice. The younger kids in the neighborhood played touch football on the side while my dad conducted practice with the big guys.

I remember one day when I was running down to the field, one of my dad's players was hiding in the bushes. He told me not to tell my dad he was hiding there, because he did not want to practice. I wondered why he would want to miss this great chance to play football, when I couldn't wait until I was old enough to play. So I went right down to the field and told my father that he was hiding in the bushes. My dad went after him and made him run lap after lap around the field. That kid was mad at me for months, but I thought I did him a favor.

My mom always tells me how she marveled at my ability to play make-believe games of baseball and football, by myself, in the side yard for hours at a time. Even at a young age I had such passion for the exhilaration of play. I was out there running, catching, throwing, and making up the rules for my own one-man game. I used to reenact the games I read about in the paper. One time I was on the empty lot playing a one-man game of football, acting out the touchdowns that were scored in the Montclair-Bloomfield game from the day before. "Hey, Mom," I yelled from the lot next to the house, "how did Montclair score their first touchdown?" She read to me from the paper, calling the details out the window. I yelled "Thanks" and continued my reenactment of the game. It was just me, the fresh air, and my beat-up football. I was in heaven, hopeful, optimistic, and loving life!

During baseball season I had a system for playing games by myself. I threw the ball against the side of the apartment house where we lived. Unfortunately, other people lived there too. One time the upstairs neighbor yelled to me. "Hey, Kevin," she bellowed, "I am trying to get some sleep! Stop throwing the ball against the house."

I said, "What are you doing sleeping? It's the middle of the day." I was unaware of something called the night shift.

"I work at night," she yelled back. "Now stop it so I can get back to sleep."

I just didn't want to leave this make-believe world of games. I mumbled to myself, "Lady, don't you know we're in extra innings? How am I going to finish my game?"

THE EVER-PRESENT PARADOX OF HOPE

Like so many things in my family, the fun of sports was a double-edged sword. My father needed sports to be the savior of the Touhey family. The badge of honor for the Touhey boys became excelling on the field. The pressure to succeed superseded the pure fun of just playing and belonging to a team.

I first felt this pressure when I was six years old. My dad decided that I showed enough promise as a baseball player to put me in a league for eight- and nine-year-olds. My siblings had to be really creative to keep my uniform from falling off. My baseball glove was so big I had to be careful when fielding a grounder, or I might leave the glove with the ball in it lying on the infield dirt.

Although I was thrilled to play in my very first official ball game, I was confused because my dad kept reminding me that if anyone asked my age, I should say I was eight years old. He had gotten me into the league by lying about my age. I always wondered why I wasn't allowed to go to practice, but as the coach's son I was going to get to play in the games. I was beginning to wonder if this was going to be as much fun as my neighborhood games, my imaginary games, or watching my cousins play.

I got the answer when I arrived at the baseball field for my first game. The other players towered over me. I was intimidated and scared, feelings I'd never experienced regarding sports. My legs wobbled as I ran out onto the field, trying to ignore the comments about the coach's son being small for his age. The very first grounder that was hit my way knocked my glove into right field. "Don't worry about it," Dad said. When it was my turn at the bat, he said, "Just get up and hit the ball."

By the time I was six years old my dad and cousins had thrown me thousands of pitches to hit. I played with kids older than me all the time. When Dad yelled, it was only at my cousins, not at me. Sports had always been fun. But suddenly things were very different. I was wearing a real uniform, like Ted Williams and Mickey Mantle; there were people watching and cheering; coaches were yelling. I was scared to death to get up to bat. Three perfectly thrown strikes whizzed right past me. My dad and Joe screamed at me in unison, "Kevin, just swing the darn bat!" Each time I was up to bat, I never took a swing. I had three strikeouts without swinging the bat, plus two errors in the field.

That night, Dad drove several of the players home. I ended up having to sit on the floor of the car. I can remember thinking that this was some sort of punishment for my less than stellar performance. But even as I felt ashamed at my performance, I also felt pretty cool since I was on a team. I had high hopes for a bright future in sports. I knew I would one day make my father proud of me.

My season ended with a repeat performance in game two. Then Dad cut me from the team. Although I was devastated, I found solace by going back to my beloved neighborhood games and my backyard make-believe.

> *Self-esteem is not measured by accomplishments or external verification. It is a very deep heart feeling of worthiness, whether you win, lose, or draw, whether you are rich or poor.*

The gift I took from this incident came from the paradox of the situation: my ability to retreat to the spirit of sports and find happiness. After that disastrous second game, I wondered why something fun felt so scary. I also wondered why people were taking this so seriously. In the years to come I would take it way too seriously, too.

Working my entire life with people in sports, I found a lot of low self-esteem masked by athletic talent. I carried my father's low self-esteem into almost every game I played and coached as a college basketball coach. It was tiring. I'm just grateful that I didn't sour on sports altogether. My failure to live up to my dad's expectations would never take away the fun of the neighborhood games and my own games.

My dad coached a lot of young people in his life. He always seemed to win. How did he affect those he coached? I know that many loved him— perhaps just those who believed in winning at all costs. I don't really know. I do know that I could not have been the only one who felt I let him down because I didn't live up to his expectations. But no matter what my dad did to me, I can honestly say that I hold no negative feelings toward him, just love.

I have a picture of me sitting on my dad's lap when I was about a year old. It reminds me of the joy that he felt in his heart looking at his son, knowing that his prayers of hope were answered. This is the father I choose to remember.

His prayers and his love for me were the greatest gifts he ever gave me. It reminds me that even in the most difficult circumstances, hope will see me through.

> *Individuals with high self-esteem look at failure as temporary. They also look at failure as an opportunity to change and challenge themselves.*

LESSON 2

DEVELOPING SELF-ESTEEM

Self-esteem is fundamentally rooted in receiving unconditional appreciation, especially in our formative years. Self-esteem is basically unconditional love for oneself. Self-esteem is a knowing at the core of our being that regardless of condition or circumstance we are worthy. Self-esteem is at the core of our belief system. Self-esteem is rooted in the fact that you love yourself regardless of what you do or do not accomplish. True heart-based self-esteem eliminates the ego's need to be arrogant.

Exercise 2

SELF-ESTEEM

1. If self-esteem is based on a core belief of self-worth, what are your most worthwhile traits?

_____

_____

_____

_____

_____

_____

_____

_____

2. Do you consider yourself a smart or talented person? If so why?
   If not, why not?

_____

_____

_____

_____

_____

_____

_____

_____

3. Do you feel worthless or inferior when you don't accomplish
   goals? How do you feel when you are not particularly produc-
   tive or successful?

_____

_____

_____

_____

_____

_____

_____

4. Do you think you are worth more than others if you work hard
   and experience success?

_____

_____

_____

_____

_____

_____

_____

_____

5. What is the difference between self-confidence and self-esteem?
   Does a person with self-confidence automatically have high self-
   esteem?

_____

_____

_____

_____

_____

_____

_____

WHAT'S YOUR STORY?

Complete this journal entry by responding to the following questions:

What have you learned about yourself in regard to your own self-esteem?

How will you apply what you have learned about developing self-esteem?

3

The Miracle of Regina Margaret Touhey

"A SISTER IS A GIFT TO THE HEART, A FRIEND
TO THE SPIRIT, A GOLDEN THREAD TO THE
MEANING OF LIFE."

— *Isadora James*

My dear little sister, Regina: You are an angel who gave me the gifts of both your life and your death. The message of your soul always lived within me. It is more vibrant and clear than ever.

I believe the gift of hope was the purpose of my sister's journey on earth. In my own journey, with Regina demonstrating hope as a foundation for growth, I was able to move from that hope to establishing a positive belief system and knowing that all is well in my world. I can now celebrate life with a spiritually based optimism that defies any negatives that find their way into my life. Moving from hope to believing to knowing was a journey that I came to realize was my responsibility. Many teachers helped along the way, but Regina was the most profound teacher I have ever had.

I believe my sister Regina came to earth to give my family an everlasting gift of hope. I have watched so many of my eight surviving siblings reach back and rely on their last bit of hope to sustain themselves in some of the toughest moments.

> *Perception is the way you see something, your frame of reference, your point of view. We view life through our perceptions. Beliefs about yourself, others, and the world around you are affected by your perceptions.*

Regina and I nearly shared the same birthdate, which my mother would have liked. I was born on August 7, 1951. Regina was born eight years later on August 8, 1959, missing the seventh by just a few hours.

The timeliness of her coming into the world cannot be overestimated. We had been evicted from our second home in Bloomfield and moved away from our large extended family to Lake Hopatcong, New Jersey. My sister Kathy and I have talked about how isolated we felt when we moved away from the whole family. Regina's birth injected new life into our circle. We were all drawn to her in a very special way. With her light brown-blond hair and blue eyes, she seemed surrounded by a light of spirit. Curiously, she made each of us feel like she loved us the most. Jeannie, as we called her, knew how to crawl into your lap and take up residence in your heart. One of the amazing things was her vocabulary. She spoke at a very young age and seemed to communicate in a very special way. That quality made you sit up and notice her.

Once, when my mon and sisters were going out, I was asked to keep an eye on Regina until they got back. I was happy to do it. I was only nine years old at the time, and Jeannie was just one. We frolicked on the floor and laughed and played together. My heart was so filled with love for her in that moment. I believe there are no coincidences in life, so we were destined to be together in this experience. We had an old record player in one of the back bedrooms. We were playing "Happy Trails" by Roy Rogers and Dale Evans. Regina was smiling and dancing, holding my hand, making me laugh.

After we played the song a few times she took me by the hand and led me to a chair in the living room. She wanted me to sit so she could curl up in my lap. I sat down in the chair and she crawled up onto my lap and into my heart. She rested her head on my chest, right next to my heart, and I felt the soft rhythmic beat of her heart in unison with mine. A powerful sense of peace flooded my entire being. We both fell into a very deep sleep that felt like a dream. The spiritual gift of calm my sister bestowed upon me quieted the distress of our lives of poverty, if only for a short while. This was more than a nap with a little sister. It was a message of peace and bliss from the old soul of a young girl.

This spiritual journey was interrupted by the joyful voices of my mom and siblings. "Look how special this is," I heard my mom say. As my sister stayed in her restful sleep, I opened my eyes to the smiling faces of my older sisters. The overwhelming love in that room transcended the family's economic situation and the simple reality of the incident: My sister had merely fallen asleep on me. That is what made Regina so special. The simplicity of sleep became a special opportunity for her to spread the light of her spirit. By taking my hand and leading me to the chair, she was showing me what having a peaceful heart meant. This soft place in the blissful heart of spirit was like a prayer.

> *Your perspective determines the feeling state and the type of energy you will use to process any situation. Your perspective determines whether that energy in motion will be positive or negative.*

I remember being on the school bus telling the driver to hurry up, that my little sister was home after a long stay in the hospital and I wanted to get home to see her. The driver stopped on the corner and I sprinted to the house. I ran in the front door and back to the kitchen where my mom was doing the laundry. Regina was sitting and eating in her high chair. I was so happy to see her! I can feel the joy of that moment as I write. I really wish I could hold her right now.

But Regina looked very ill, so sickly that I hardly recognized her. She was very pale. Her eyes seemed to be bugging out of her head. It was shocking to behold. I looked at my mom, who said nothing. She wouldn't make eye contact with me and her entire demeanor was sad and scared. I looked back at Regina and kissed her all over her face and head. She giggled in delight. I was so happy to see her, my heart could've burst out of my chest.

"Hello, Jeannie," I said as she giggled in delight at seeing me. She was smiling, but I could see she did not feel well. I began to feel sad and afraid like my mom. I turned to my mother, asking, "Mom, come on, Regina does not look like herself, is she going to be okay?"

"Yes, honey, she will be fine," my mom responded. "You know, Kev, she just got home from the hospital. Give her a few days and she will be back to her old self."

I turned back to Regina and said, "I love you, little one," as I tickled her under her chin. She shrieked a delighted, "No, no, no, Kevin," in response. As I snuggled up on her neck I could see the dried blood on her ear. She often bled from her nose and ears. No matter what Mom said, I knew she would not be okay. I knew she would not be with us much longer. I was feeling bereft already.

Within a month Regina's condition worsened. She developed lumps on her back and had to go back to the hospital. I never saw her alive again.

After Regina went back into the hospital, I vividly remember hearing the phone ring. My mother came down the steps after hanging up. I had never seen her look so sad. Mom said, "It was the hospital calling. They said that Jeannie was not feeling very well. Dad is going to visit her." My father was out of work and we had no car. So when that call came telling us that Regina was dying, my dad scrambled to borrow a friend's car. By the time he got there, my sister had died, alone. I can't even imagine the depth of his pain as he held his dead daughter or the sorrow he experienced in that moment as his world fell apart. My dad just held her. Holding his daughter, he must have been ashamed he could not get there in time to say goodbye.

I know that Regina's spirit restored hope within me so that I could forgive my father. I have. I can tell you that the love I feel for him as I imagine him holding my sister and saying goodbye comes from the deepest recesses of my soul.

My sister Kathleen told me the following story in November 2006, crying as she spoke. Kathy had a very profound experience with Regina during her last stay in the hospital. She'd gone to the hospital to visit Regina in my mother's place. Kathy told me it was her only visit to the hospital the whole time Regina was hospitalized. Regina was about to give the same kind of spiritual gift to Kathy as she had when we took a nap together.

When it was time for Kathy to leave, Regina took Kathy's hand and walked to the door with her sister, who was also her godmother. As Regina walked her to the door, she kept asking Kathy not to leave, but to take her home. Regina did not want to die alone in the hospital, yet she knew that would happen. She wanted Kathy to take her home to be with the family to die. She chose Kathy to receive this message. She held Kathy's hand as they walked down the hall toward the exit. When Kathy walked through the door, it closed behind her. Regina pressed her hand against the door as Kathy left, the way she always had when Kathy, Maureen, and Eileen arrived home from school. She was so excited to see them that she would greet them and press her hand up against the front door for them to touch.

This was the first time Kathy had told me her story. She felt helpless since she could not bring Regina home. But I believe Regina was relaying a spiritual message: "I am special, Kathleen, my dear sister, and you are special too. Kathy, I will miss you here on earth."

This story still haunts my sister. I think Regina was telling her she loved her and wanted to be with her brothers and sisters before she left the physical plane. Regina already knew that she was going to die alone. She wanted to come home to die and was trying to convey that message to Kathy.

I felt such love for my sister Kathleen, and I felt her pain as she revisited the scene.

> *Very often, perspective is tainted by expectations. The expectations that we have of ourselves, others, and situations often produce negative feeling states if those expectations are not met. Expectations are an emotional investment in our own point of view.*

I believe Kathy can heal her feelings by tapping into the special way Regina communicated with us. Kathy may not have been able to do that at the age of sixteen, but I hope now she can view that loving interaction with our sister in a new light. I truly believe that each member of the Touhey family had one of these experiences with Regina. Eileen had numerous encounters with her, and Maureen told me that Eileen and Regina connected in a very special way.

I asked Maureen about any special encounters she herself had with Regina. She shared this story with me.

When Regina first became ill, it seemed to my parents that she could not shake an awful cold she had. One afternoon while Regina was upstairs sleeping, Maureen and my mom were watching TV. A show about different kinds of diseases came on, and at some point they started to discuss leukemia. Our family had no knowledge of leukemia, and no doctor had even mentioned the possibility that Regina might have leukemia, not a cold. But Maureen turned to my mom when the leukemia segment was over and said "Mom, that's what Regina has." It was no coincidence that she received that message. It flowed energetically from Regina.

One of the more compelling stories comes from my brother Patrick, who did not even know Regina. He related the following story to me.

"For the life of me I cannot remember what compelled me to go to Regina's grave, but nonetheless, I went to see her. I remember asking the graveyard attendant where I could find her. He told me there was no gravestone with her name, only a number. When I went to the number I remember feeling so sad and disconnected from my sister. I promised Regina that day that she would have a gravestone with her name.

"I went back to the attendant and told him that I wanted to place a gravestone with Regina's name at her site. He told me I could not do it without a consent form from Regina's parents. After a few days had passed, I went home to Dover and talked to Mom about it and asked her if I could get Regina a gravestone. She said it would be fine with her, but she did not think Dad would agree. I remember going into the living room to ask Dad, and feeling paralyzed with fear. He told me it would be okay.

"I went ahead and purchased the stone. I remember the day I was informed that it had arrived. I went back to the gravesite to talk to Regina. When I first saw her name, I broke down in tears because it was the first time in my life that I felt connected to my sister. I knew at that time that I loved her and that she was special.

"My soul is connected to Regina. I did not know it then, but Regina wanted me to know she was with me. As you say, there are no coincidences. At this time in my life I had almost one year of sobriety. By no longer numbing myself with alcohol, maybe I allowed myself to have that very special encounter with my sister."

We moved across the lake to a house in Mount Arlington. By then my parents knew Regina had leukemia and were still in shock.

That last visit home by Regina turned into the most profound experience of my life. The story would seem to end with her death, but it did not. In fact, for most of my life I denied the events that followed during those terrible days.

For forty-five years I thought that things had happened as I describe in the next few paragraphs. The reality of what really transpired was buried along with the other memories of my dear sister.

One day shortly before she was to go back into the hospital, I was sitting on the floor at the foot of my bed with my back against the wall, crying. I had been thinking about a time a year earlier when I watched Regina while the rest of the family was out. She had fallen asleep in my arms. I was remembering the calm rhythm of her breathing and the beating of her heart.

As I was in this reverie of sorrow, Regina walked into the room. In a perfectly enunciated sentence, with clear, precise delivery, she said, "Kevin, don't worry. Everything will be all right."

I understood what she meant, too. Not that she would be all right; just that everything would be all right—everything. Although her vocabulary was advanced, this was way beyond even her normal verbal skills. With that simple sentence coming from the most spiritual depths of her soul, Regina was telling me to never lose hope, that no matter what, everything would be all right. The "no matter what" in there is always the hope that things will turn around. I can still see her standing in that doorway of the downstairs bathroom that was accessible to the bedroom I shared with my brothers, Brian and Dennis. She looked so beautiful in that moment, not at all like the sick girl I had kissed all up.

After that experience with her, I have no recollection of any further interaction with her in human form. That always baffled me. Why could-n't I remember seeing her after that day?

Afraid of what people might think about this encounter, I did not share it with anyone for many years. Finally I mentioned it to my sister Eileen, who also had a special relationship with Regina. "Maybe she wasn't using words," Eileen said. "Perhaps she was just communicating a message from her spirit."

This was an epiphany—I had never before thought of this encounter in such terms. The mystery seemed to be solved.

Then, on a cold night in December 2005, I had another epiphany. I was taking a class sponsored by the Center for Conscious Living in Moorestown, New Jersey. The class was called Foundations for Living and was being taught by Rev. Dr. Carol Lawson, the founding minister. The topic that night was our view of death and dying. As we shared our experiences, I listened very intently and very quietly. A whole new level of self-awareness was pouring over me. One woman, Jane, spoke of her mother's difficult pregnancy with her. In fact, Jane's mother had been told that a pregnancy would be dangerous for her health, and she was worried that things were not going right with the pregnancy. One night as she lay in bed, her deceased mother appeared at the foot of the bed and told her that everything would be all right.

That's when I felt myself kind of leave the room, although I was there physically. Another student talked about her profound experiences in meditation. She'd connected in a very real way with her own mother, with whom she had been very close. My recollection of the encounter with Regina so many years ago began to expand. But as I had done many times before, I held the memory back. I could not raise my hand to tell my story.

At the close of each class a song was played. But this time the music would not cue up. During the delay, Rev. Dr. Carol asked if anyone else wanted to share. Finally, I raised my hand. I was ready to tell what really happened the night of the funeral.

My mother didn't let me go to Regina's funeral. Afterward, when she got home, I asked her if I could hold the Mass card. She gave me the card and I held it to my heart as if I was actually holding my baby sister. I cried so hard, wanting only to feel my connection with her. I told her that I missed her and to come back. There had been an incident after the funeral where my father nearly killed my uncle, and I was scared. Any measure of family cohesion seemed broken. To my little boy's eyes, the Touhey family was in serious trouble.

I realized now that it was the day *after* the funeral when I sat at the end of my bed. The night before I'd been crying so hard and moaning "Regina, please come home," so loud and sad that my mom came back and took the Mass card away from me and lovingly said, "Kevin, go to sleep now." I shared with the class that I now knew it was on the day after the funeral that I got up and found the Mass card again. I cradled that card as I had cradled her face on her last visit. I cried pitifully and couldn't seem to stop. Since I was not allowed to go to the wake or funeral, I had never said a final good-bye to my little sister. My mom said I was too young to see my sister that way, too young to understand death or a funeral. She thought it best for me to remember Regina's last trip home and how she giggled when I kissed her all up. Maybe she was right.

I was holding the Mass card to my heart as I sat on the floor at the end of the bed. Then my dear little sister Regina came in. She spoke so clearly and looked so beautiful, not sick at all. She had a light of peace and love around her. The reason was, she had already passed the day before. I'd felt hopeless and she wanted me to know everything would be all right.

Through the years I buried all those memories so far down inside that I couldn't sort out what had truly transpired. I didn't connect with the experience at all until that moment in class as the others spoke up. The day after class, I called my sister Maureen to ask her about the dress Regina was wearing when she visited me. I described the dress to my sister and she told me that I had described it perfectly. She said my Aunt Laya had made the dress for Regina. She'd never worn the dress until she was buried in it.

> *Rather than accepting your beliefs, question them in a way that will empower you to seek new information and experiences and change your perception.*

My sister gave me a lesson of hope in the direst human situation of all, the fight for her life. She fought that fight with a smile on her little face and spiritual laughter in her huge heart. She was not exemplifying the hope that she would survive the terrible disease that ravaged her body. She was not concerned with that. The whole purpose of her human experience was to show pragmatically how we can change our perception of what is transpiring in our lives. Good or bad, we can then deal with it from a foundation of hope.

I have always prayed to Regina. Now I do it differently. I know that my prayers to my sister have always been answered. She always led me back to hope no matter what I prayed about or wanted to happen in my life. What I know now is that the answers lay right inside of me, in my soul, where God lives.

Most of the time, I wasn't aware my prayers were being answered. I had too much ego in the way to receive the message as it was being given. The message is, "Kevin, everything will be all right in your world; always remain hopeful. Just believe and know that all is well in your world. Find your way back to your optimism. Get in touch with your soul."

All human beings are here for that reason. It's just that most humans do not remember why their soul chose their particular human experience. They forget to make the conscious connection to an entity greater than their own ego. We do not remember to connect with the greatness that lies inside all of us. It's the connection to the place where God lives in each of our souls. Mahatma Gandhi, Martin Luther King Jr., and my sister Regina made that connection. It is our mission on earth to make that connection too. The soul looks for a spot to manifest on earth to do the most good. The soul looks for a place to make the biggest contribution to others. When each of us realizes this, it sheds a light on our life and gives it a purpose that is truly God-sent. The human beings who seem to be the embodiment of spirit are those who have made this connection. That is why we are so drawn to them. My sister Regina was such a person.

I was blessed to have had this direct experience at a very young age. The phenomenon of spiritual manifestation into human form in the life and death of my dear sister was such a profound blessing. She bestowed the spirit of hope upon the entire Touhey family. I wasn't always consciously aware that the gift was there for the taking. She demonstrated for me the expectation that something desirable was just around the corner if I just kept hope alive. I am now ready to fully accept her gift without reservation and move into my soul connection and to connect with the God that lives in me. I now adopt a life of absolute optimism based on the knowledge that all is right in the world of Kevin Touhey. It is time to fulfill my soul's desire to contribute to the ultimate good of this human experience.

Because of my reconnection to my sister's message, I see that I have chosen this human experience exactly as it is. My soul chose to come into this human experience to do the most good possible. I haven't always lived that credo. Sometimes I have strayed very far from my soul's mission here on earth. That's when my life has been the most painful. But there is no turning back now. I am fully connected to the fact that I chose this life. So if you choose it, use it to do the most good. That's what Regina did.

It is now a matter of how I choose to contribute to the overall good that will help me make my way back to my soul's Source, my higher power, the God who resides in my heart. Regina's death, not her life, was always the focal point of discussions in our family. Her legacy was a special girl's death. The discussions were always centered on how special she was and what a shame it was she died so young. It was truly the spirit of her living and her giving that was the most profound result of her short visit on earth. Regina's life was a reflection of hope, joy, faith, love, and happiness. But all these years I have had the emphasis on the wrong part of her being—her death.

In her last stay in the hospital before she died, she played tricks on the kids and nurses that gave the whole floor of dying children and their caretakers a chance to laugh. This little eighteen-month-old sprite would get down from her bed and go around the hospital ward and take all the other children's slippers. She hid them in the closet so the kids would have to come to her room and get their slippers. I know my sister just wanted to bring some joy to a dire situation. That is true spirit. Regardless of her own condition, her motivation was to bring happiness to those around her.

I remember my father telling me near the end of his life that he could never get over the death of Regina. He said her death ruined his relationship with the church and with God. He just could not understand how God could have taken her away.

I don't think God is hovering around deciding who should die and who should live. I wish that my dad could have tapped into Regina's life, not her death. If he'd stopped asking, "Why, God, did you take my little daughter?" and instead used the special gift of Regina's life to do the most good, the unbearable pain of his loss might have been eased. That takes extraordinary faith. I am writing these words without judgment; I have no idea what state I would be in if one of my children died. But just maybe he would've discovered God residing right inside himself. He might have been able to make sense of the purity of Regina's spiritual intention to bring hope to this poor struggling family.

My sister Kathy told me, "Dad was unable to pass this particular test of his faith and hopefulness." Perhaps she is right.

> *Our perceptions create personal limitations if they are inaccurate. Perceptions are like glasses. When you have misperceptions about yourself, others, or just life in general, it is like wearing distorted lenses. Those distortions affect everything you see and experience.*

It would be twenty-seven years before I truly mourned Regina's death, let alone told anyone about my encounter with her. To tell anyone how she sounded like an adult when she spoke to me and how she didn't look sick, just beautiful, might have been puzzling. Finally, I understand. I know deep in the place where God lives that what Regina Margaret Touhey said forty-five years ago is true. No matter what my earthly circumstances, everything will be all right. My life is now a Miracle of Optimism.

LESSON 3

PERCEPTIONS

"Whether we're aware of it or not,
an energy economy game is going on
inside of us throughout life. Our inner
experience over the course of each
day includes thousands of thoughts,
feelings, and impressions that directly
impact our energy level."

— *Doc Childre*

For many years my perceptions about situations in my life were based on the views of others. There's no need to make a value judgment about the intentions of other people; you just need to know you have been affected by their perceptions. For example, it was my mother's perception that I was too young to go to my sister's funeral, too young to process her death. Her perception changed the way I looked at my sister's visit to me. I believed that if I was too young to go to the funeral, how was I going to trust the events that transpired after Regina's death?

Additionally, my perceptions of my father and mother and how much they loved the children in the family may be very different from my siblings' perceptions.

The intent of this exercise is to examine your perceptions as they exist at this particular moment of your life. It will help you take a new look at how you view the circumstances of your present-day life. Greater awareness of your perceptions will also give you greater awareness of your present energy state. Your energy for living a positive life is the foundation for optimistic living.

It is important to know which negative feelings you are carrying around on a daily basis. Research shows that anger, frustration, worry, fear, jealousy, resentment, and nervousness affect your ability to think clearly, act efficiently, and communicate effectively. Negative emotion affects your ability to live life with enthusiasm and optimism. You cannot feel all the negative feelings you may uncover in this exercise and feel positive at the same time.

The first step toward living an optimistic life is to examine your situations and circumstances.

Exercise 3

PERCEPTIONS

In this exercise, you will examine positive and negative energy sources. Referring to the list of feelings on the next page, respond to the following questions and list the feelings you have.

Note: By commitments I mean family, education, career or employment situations, as well as intimate relationships. For example, you may examine the commitment of what it feels like to work in your career or job. In the first part of this exercise we're not examining the people involved in your work situation, just the situation itself. The next exercise will examine the people within the commitment.

How do you feel about your commitments?

1. In what ways do your commitments affect you and your feeling state? Identify those feelings from the list and write them down.
2. Next, examine how the people connected with those commitments make you feel. This may include parents, spouse, siblings, coaches, teachers, etc.

Feelings

- Not enough time
- Rushed
- Moody (lots of ups and downs)
- Tired
- Bored; apathetic
- Depressed
- Quick to get irritated or frustrated
- Anxious
- Short-tempered
- Angry
- Unloved
- Disliked
- Unfulfilled
- Overwhelmed
- Disheartened
- Racing thoughts
- Tense

To live an optimistic life, start right now and become aware of how you are viewing your situations and circumstances.

The goal is to transform your feeling states to positive ones like the following: Calm, confident, happy, joyful, enthusiastic, appreciative, esteemed, and filled with grace.

WHAT'S YOUR STORY?

Journal about what you've learned about your view of life. Examine where your perceptions may have originated.

_____

_____

_____

_____

_____

_____

_____

_____

_____

_____

_____

_____

_____

_____

PART
2
INCLUSION

"WE DARE NOT FORGET THAT INCLUSION,
NOT EXCLUSION, IS THE WAY OF GRACE."
— *Denise Ackerman, South African theologian*

My definition of inclusion is that feeling deep inside that you are part of something larger than yourself. In my life I've had many experiences that helped me draw the conclusion that I was part of a bigger whole. My score on the 1-to-10 scale for feeling inclusion is a 7 or 8. The reason my score is high is because my family, the community, the neighborhoods, and the athletic teams I belonged to contributed to that feeling of inclusion.

I have so many stories that exemplify my feeling of inclusion. In an earlier chapter I shared how much love I received from my sisters and parents both before and after my birth. I was born into hope and internalized the feeling state of safety that comes with the protection of being part of the whole.

4

The Miracle of Family

"THE FAMILY IS THE NUCLEUS OF CIVILIZATION."

— *William James Durant*

We lived in Nutley in the barracks until I was four, and then we moved to Newark Avenue in Bloomfield. It was great living there and we stayrd for four and a half years. I recently found out from my mom that we were asked to leave because we couldn't pay the rent.

While we lived in Bloomfield, I was in the same grade and class as my cousin Betty Ann. I attended Sacred Heart School in Bloomfield from kindergarten through second grade. I was a very good student during that period; I remember being placed in an advanced reading group with my cousin Betty Ann during the second grade. I was on the Sacred Heart stage with her, singing "The Good Ship Lollipop," at our kindergarten graduation ceremony. It felt wonderful to have all my relatives watching, right there in the audience. They lived so close by that I felt surrounded by my extended family. After all the years of moving from place to place, this was blissful!

It was so cool that Betty Ann was with me every day. In addition, her brothers Joe and Rob were always at our house. They lived right down the street. Their mother Mary was my father's sister. The consistency that came from having them right there and feeling part of this large family was like glue holding me together.

When we lived on Newark Avenue in Bloomfield, my mother could take my brothers and me out the front door and onto a bus for a short ride to my Grandmother Mimi's house in Nutley, the house where my mom grew up after she moved back to New Jersey from Virginia. The roots of my mom's childhood were right in that house.

There were many Sundays when the whole family got in the car for the short drive to Nutley to visit Mimi. There was a big tower owned by AT&T that was just down the street from Mimi's house. When we saw the tower we would say, "Hey, there is Mimi's tower," as though she owned it. "We're almost there." Often a visit to Mimi's house meant that my Mom's sister Agnes would be there with her family. Agnes's husband, Carl, visited with my dad, Cousin Linda visited with my sisters, and Brian, Dennis, Cousin Tom, and I just ran all over the entire neighborhood with absolute glee. We had such fun! When my mother's father, Grandfather Eggert (also called Pop-Pop) was alive, he hid our Easter baskets in the woods down the street from the house. I was very young, but I remember all of us running into the woods looking for the goodies. My sisters have told the Easter basket story many times over the years. I never get tired of hearing it.

I vividly remember when it got late in the day on those Sunday visits. Sometimes we stayed a little later and watched *The Wonderful World of Disney* on TV. When it was over, we went home. The feeling of belonging to something was very high on the scale during those times. It was important to have that anchor.

To this day I have such strong emotional memories of those times. Whenever I hear Disney music, see an old Disney movie, or take my own children to Walt Disney World, those emotions surface in me. I can feel my own roots. A warm feeling comes over me, along with some melancholy feelings. I truly associate Disney with my cousins Linda and Tom and our Sunday visits to Mimi's house.

My father's sister, Aunt Mary Carter, lived right down the street from us in Bloomfield. Her sons, Rob and Joe, were a central part of my upbringing until we moved when I was nine years old. Recently my cousin Rob and I had a visit. He told me, "Kevin, all I knew was that the Carters and Touheys were going to have fun with Uncle Jimmy." That was true whenever he and Joe were visiting us, whether we played ball at Wright's field or just hung out. Having them right down the street was great! In the 1950s, the whole neighborhood was family. By the age of five, I was walking down the street and crossing Franklin Street to Aunt Mary's house with no problem. The neighbors up and down the street kept an eye on me. I can still picture them out on their porches saying hello or asking if my mom knew where I was. I felt safe, surrounded by one big extended family. Connecting with people is so important.

My father's mother, Grandma Touhey, lived with the Carters. My family went to the Carters for visits where the central theme for the boys was sports. If we weren't playing a sport, we were watching a game on TV. My fondest memories are of watching the Red Sox versus the Yankees with my brothers, my dad, and Uncle Clemont, Rob and Joe's dad. It always was so much fun! There was a pretty even split between those of us who liked the Sox and those who cheered for the Yanks. So we laughed and carried on as we watched the game. There was lots of ribbing, depending on whose team was winning. The score on the inclusion scale of 1 to 10 went way up from events like these.

Aunt Mary occasionally hosted large get-togethers that included my Aunt Bridget, one of my father's sisters, her husband, Ed, and all of the cousins. We had a ball! There is a picture of my brother Dennis dancing and everyone enjoying his entertainment as we listened to music on the old record player.

> *It is important to be aware that many of our beliefs about ourselves are based on how we view the past.*

PLAYING: POWERFUL SIBLING BONDS OF INCLUSION

"YOU CAN DISCOVER MORE ABOUT A PERSON IN AN HOUR OF PLAY THAN IN A YEAR OF CONVERSATION."

— *Plato*

Living at the lake wasn't all bad for us. One of the truly wonderful things that happened was that my love for the water and swimming grew. When we lived in Bloomfield, we had taken day trips to the lake, loading up the car with a picnic lunch and swimming all day. We jumped off the dock for hours at a time. Now we just walked down the street and there was the lake. Despite our circumstances and living conditions, playing with my brothers and sisters formed an indelible bond between us. My father loved the water and he passed that on to me. Being near the water still brings me great joy and peace. I can sit there for hours and just be.

I also credit my mother with nurturing our sibling bond. She always made sure that we looked out for one another. I believe she knew instinctively that poverty could have a way of separating us and making us turn on one another. She was adamant about making sure we included each other. I remember while we lived at the lake there was a celebration at the firehouse for the Fourth of July. There was a fair and the firemen were giving out free ice cream. I helped myself to the free stuff and made my way home.

I came in the door and told my mom about the fair and the free ice cream. She asked why I hadn't brought any for my brothers who were sick and had stayed at home. When I told her I hadn't thought about that, she responded that I should never leave my brothers out, even if they were not around. She sent me back to get free ice cream for them. When I told her it would melt, she said to run as fast as I could so I could preserve most of it. I went to get their goodies and ran back home as fast as I could. My mom had taught me another lesson in inclusion.

Playing was free. My five brothers and I bonded through play. No toys were needed. We played in the woods and the sticks became guns for Revolutionary War. An empty oatmeal box was a kicking tee. A worn-out football, a bat, and a ball were all we needed to keep us busy for hours. Even though we were competitive (and I cheated in order to win the games we played!), we loved each other and had a lot of fun. We frolicked in an abandoned house at the edge of the woods and made up games that occupied us for hours. Play was the way we escaped the pain of poverty. It was an important tool for survival, and it gave us the feeling of being included in something bigger than ourselves.

The amount of time Brian, Dennis, Timothy, Patrick, Michael, and I spent together playing was indescribably special. It gave us a feeling of safety that we got nowhere else. The bond we formed helped us develop the feeling of believing in something bigger than ourselves. As a unit of brothers, we were much larger than we could be as individuals. I loved that time together. I think it encouraged me to stay hopeful on a very deep spiritual level. It was the silver lining in trying times and kept the fires of hope burning in my heart.

Sometime Brian, Dennis, and I collected empty soda bottles to redeem at the store for two cents each. On one particular day we were on our way to the store to get money to buy penny candy. On the way up the hill we were stopped by a gang of older boys who wanted to take our bottles. I was holding the half dozen bottles we had found and the older boys made a move toward me to steal them. I told them the bottles were ours, trying to talk them out of taking them. Just then my five-year-old brother, Brian, shoved one of the bigger boys and told them to leave us alone. The others took note and backed away. I felt my little brother was pretty tough, and I wasn't alone.

This little band of dirty, poor brothers had kept the big boys at bay. We triumphantly went on our way to the corner store, cashed in our bottles for twelve cents' worth of penny candy, and feasted as we rehashed the story of Brian's bravery, laughing all the way home. The richest part of that excursion was that the incident deepened the bond between us. We learned to stick together.

> *It is absolutely possible to live a happy and abundant life. It is possible to tap into a power that all humans have to create empowering beliefs that make your life completely joyful to behold. That power is rooted in an attitude of appreciation and gratitude.*

ME AND DAD: A POWERFUL STORY OF INCLUSION

One of the main ways I bonded with my father and became an indelible part of him has its roots in Mount Arlington. It was in Mount Arlington that he first took me to some of the jobs he held. Having me with him provided a level of comfort that he didn't understand, but he felt more secure. I understand now that he felt unsafe by himself. The world scared him. Having eleven mouths to feed overwhelmed him. In a real sense, all he had was his family. What a paradox! We were all he had, yet he was too dysfunctional to provide for us. The only human connections he had were with his family and especially with me, his eldest son. It was as though I was his talisman to ward off his own fear. Many times in our adult years, my siblings and I discussed this and wondered why he took this little kid to work with him. The explanation is clear to me now. He had the same basic human need to belong to something larger than himself. My presence helped to satisfy that need.

My dad's family of origin hadn't provided any consistency in his life either. I doubt he really ever felt appreciated. He was really trying to create what he lacked as a child. In his adult life, in spite of all the self-inflicted troubles he experienced, his one anchor was his family. It did not matter that there was major dysfunction within that family. On the conscious level he showed a lot of anger and frustration. On a deeper level he was a scared little boy whose own father had abandoned him. Consequently this very big man needed to hold this very small boy— me—close to him like a security blanket.

The scariest job my dad took me to was at the docks of Port Newark. He had a job as a security officer, driving around the waterfront looking for any signs of trouble. I got down on the floor of the car as he walked out onto the pier to make sure there were no bad guys. I did not enjoy going with him on that job.

I continued accompanying him to work over the years. I held down nine-hour shifts with him at car dealerships. I am sure his coworkers wondered what this guy was doing bringing his kid to work with him all day. I played make-believe in the cars, pretending I was driving cross-country, delivering milk, or being a garbageman. When I played garbageman, sometimes I gathered all the sales brochures and put them in the back of the "garbage truck," better known as the trunk of the car. I can hear the salesman yelling, "Hey, what happened to the Ford Fairlane brochures? I have a customer here!" I put them back before I reached the "landfill" with my trunk full of "garbage."

I used my imagination to provide the entertainment to while the hours away. I remember when my dad worked at Dougherty Ford in Morris Plains, New Jersey. Sometimes I went to work with him on Saturdays, when one of the salesmen always brought in great donuts. I got to pick whichever one I wanted. I'd go off by myself and eat that donut until it was nothing more than a sweet memory. On one occasion, I had an abscessed tooth and I knew I should be careful eating that donut. A small piece got stuck in my tooth and I was in pain the entire nine hours I was with my dad. I didn't say a word about my tooth hurting. I couldn't go to the dentist anyway. This was just another symptom of being poor.

A fond memory from travels with Dad was the occasional treat of eating lunch at Rod's Ranch House. I ate my first turkey club sandwich at Rod's.

My dad worked for a brief while for Mt. Fern Dairy, delivering milk while we lived in Mount Arlington. It is a bit ironic that a few years later when we moved to Dover, the Little League team I played for was Mt. Fern Dairy. My mom woke me up in the middle of the night and I went with Dad on his milk route. We had a routine down pat and I was assigned certain houses. I ran up to the porches and placed the milk, eggs, or orange juice in the little metal boxes that were on every front porch in that era.

I really loved being with my dad on those milk runs. It was at these times that I felt the innocence of the deep love he had for me. There was no yelling or uneasiness during those early-morning moments driving around before anyone was awake. It was just me and my father riding around in this truck stuffed to the gills with good stuff to eat and drink. I'm sure it was a temporary break from the pressures at home for my dad, just him and his first-born son, Kevin, on the road. Ironically, we delivered food to families on the route that we couldn't afford at home ourselves.

The really cool thing about the milk route was that there was always a time when my dad pulled over and told me it was time for a reward for all my hard work. Then he broke out the chocolate milk. Just as it was with the donuts and the turkey club, it was truly a magical moment when my dad handed over that dark, creamy treat as a thank-you for being with him. Mt. Fern Dairy chocolate milk was true nectar of the gods and pure heaven on earth!

This pattern of taking me to work continued for years. I did not go every day, but I accompanied him often. The days my dad seemed to need me most were when the poverty we lived in felt the worst to him. I totally understand that today. I am so grateful I provided a measure of safety and comfort to a man who experienced so little of it.

As a college freshman at the County College of Morris (CCM), I helped my father get the last job he would ever hold. It was also the longest stretch of time that he ever worked at one job. I believe he worked there for thirteen years. I asked my coach, Jack Martin, if he would hire my dad as the equipment manager. He said yes, and the rest, as they say, is history. It turned out to be Dad's longest stretch because in spite of my father's erratic behavior, Coach Martin refused to fire him. I once asked Coach why, in spite of that behavior, he never let my father go. He responded by saying he knew there were a lot of mouths to feed in the Touhey household and he could put up with my father's antics rather than penalize the whole family. The positive impact of that decision cannot be fully measured in words.

My involvement with my dad in his employment situations spanned a very long time, from the age of ten or eleven until I went to college. At CCM, my work-study job was in the equipment room and my boss was James Touhey. Instead of pulling over on the side of the road and drinking chocolate milk or eating donuts and turkey clubs, my dad and I went on walks around the campus. We talked a lot on those walks, and it felt really normal. The day he died, I went for a walk at CCM, the same route he and I had taken so many years ago. It felt good.

A positive, empowering belief system WILL attract the life you want to live! Your positive belief system provides the power to continuously create your vision.

DAD'S COACHING AND COUSIN JOE: A BROADER SCOPE OF INCLUSION

During our time in Glen Ridge, my father coached football at Immaculate Conception High School (IC), and that was fun for me. My sisters Maureen and Kathleen were students at the high school and my cousin Joseph was an athletic hero at the school. He played three sports, was popular with all the girls, and took me under his wing.

With my dad as the freshman football coach, I got to know all his players. The high school was attached to the grammar school by a small corridor that led to the shared cafeteria. I often talked to the athletes during lunchtime. I was probably a bit of a novelty to them. I was the water boy for the football team and went to all the practices and games, so I was with the high school guys a lot. I hung out in the locker room and listened to all the dirty jokes, and my cousin picked me up in his Ford Falcon for all the home games. I was a big deal by my own standards.

I was also the bat boy for the baseball team and sometimes the ball boy for basketball. Many a day during the school year, my famous cousin Joe came into my fifth-grade class and got me out of class to go to one game or another. My chest swelled with pride when the hero of IC athletics waltzed into the classroom and charmed the good sister into letting me go just one more time. It was great to gather my stuff from that cloakroom and run out the door. It was fun riding on the bus with my hero cousin and all my buddies who were five to eight years older than me.

During the entire school year, while the fifth graders were going home and doing their homework or getting together to play, I was going to practice. Football was especially fun because my younger brothers Brian and Dennis often were there. My dad and Joe were always there. We played with the tackling dummies or threw the football. Two of the varsity coaches, Mr. Joe Gravy and Mr. Don Panara, always kidded with us. They loved to see us running around the field.

The pain of my sister's death seemed to fade in those moments. It was definitely where my father seemed most at peace. Dad had coached Joe, the son of his most beloved sister Mary, in various sports since he was small. Even as a little kid I felt that coaching and being on the field was Dad's sanctuary from the pain. It gave me hope that maybe everything would be all right.

After basketball games, my cousin took me to Grunnings Soda Shop on Bloomfield Avenue. He gave me some money and I sat at the soda fountain counter eating ice cream while he entertained four or five girls in a booth, telling stories. That's where I got the idea that I could be a ladies' man and began my courtship of a senior cheerleader, Joann Morris. I began to wait for her after school and walk her to the corner where she caught the bus. I was really in love. One time she held my hand while we walked to her bus. She was probably thinking what a nice little boy this cousin of Joe Carter was. I thought I was dating a senior in high school.

I was always at the playground designated for the high-school students. My cousin's wife Susan, who was also a student at IC, told me recently how she loved to watch Sister try to chase me from the high-school playground back to the playground where I really belonged.

LESSON 4

DEVELOPING A POSITIVE BELIEF SYSTEM

It is imperative to be aware of what you believe to be true about yourself. All of the lessons to be learned from reading this book are predicated on self-awareness. I know that many of the beliefs you have about yourself are based on the messages you have received from other people.

I remember a foreman on one of my summer jobs telling me I needed more "stick-to-it-ive-ness." I looked at him like he was crazy. I knew very well that was a lesson I had down pat! In that case, I simply disregarded what he believed to be true about me. But many beliefs that I adopted as truth weren't true at all.

It is impossible to live a vibrant, happy life without developing an optimistic belief about what is possible for you in your life. What you believe about yourself can lead to either a life filled with joy and happiness or a life of striving to overcome erroneous perceptions of personal weaknesses.

Every person has the power to develop a positive belief system, no matter what others have taught him to the contrary. You can develop a more empowering system of beliefs that will embolden you to expect a life filled with all the abundance you desire. You can use this positive belief system to break the shackles of disempowering messages you have received about who you are. You can then develop feelings about yourself that propel you to take actions that assure your happiness. If you have beliefs that are holding you back, it is time to question the validity of those beliefs.

Exercise 4

YOUR BELIEF SYSTEM

1. What beliefs about yourself may be holding you back or disempowering you?

_____

_____

_____

_____

_____

2. What beliefs about yourself move you forward and empower you?

_____

_____

_____

_____

3. In what way has your life been affected by both disempowering and empowering beliefs? List three ways for each.

_____

_____

_____

_____

_____

_____

4. Name three people who have contributed to your belief system. Did they model empowering or disempowering beliefs?

_____

_____

_____

_____

_____

_____

5. What would it take to eliminate all your disempowering beliefs and replace them with empowering beliefs?

_____

_____

_____

_____

_____

_____

WHAT'S YOUR STORY?

Journal about how your belief system has impacted your life in both positive and negative ways.

_____

_____

_____

_____

_____

_____

_____

_____

_____

_____

_____

_____

_____

_____

_____

_____

_____

_____

_____

5

The Miracle of Dover

"Life's a voyage that's homeward bound."
— *Herman Melville*

I am so grateful that my family moved to Dover, New Jersey, in 1962. I was eleven years old, but I already felt much older. I lived in the house at 167 Penn Avenue until 1973, when I was twenty-one years old and got married for the first time. As I write this, my eighty-four-year-old mother still lives there, along with my eldest sister, Kathleen. Recently Kathy told me she felt such relief when we landed in Dover that night in 1962. She remembers sitting on a mattress on the floor with Maureen and Eileen and telling them we'd all be all right. The Touhey family had finally stopped moving.

During the first eleven years of my life we had moved eight times. That first night in our new home, I ate pizza and lay down on the mattress with my brothers Brian and Dennis. I immediately felt at home and safe. This was our house, thanks to the generosity and kindness of Mr. Ryerson and the inspiration of Regina.

My mother and father had met Mr. and Mrs. Ryerson when their son was in the hospital at the same time as Regina and formed a friendship. I can remember Mr. Ryerson visiting with my father when we lived in Mount Arlington. I rode around in an Army jeep with them (Mr. Ryerson was in the Army Reserve) and they stopped at a few bars. Ultimately, they ended up at the bar across the street from the house, the same bar and deli where I would go to ask for food.

It is such a divine miracle that they met, with Regina's illness as the catalyst. The move to Dover grounded our family. We were on our feet for the first time in a long time. Of course, we soon had as many financial problems as ever. We were going to need the same kind of perseverance and

faith to get through. But there was a difference this time. We were not going to be evicted from our home for not paying the rent; we no longer had a landlord. Mr. Ryerson had transferred the mortgage to my parents! My mother borrowed $2,000 from her mother for a down payment and the deed was transferred. They made the transaction and went to the local bank, where Mr. Ryerson was a customer in good standing, and informed them there was a new owner at 167 Penn Avenue. I think some of the financial moves made by the Touhey family put into motion a flurry of new banking regulations for the next generation of borrowers!

In his latest book about inspiration, Dr. Wayne Dyer says there are no coincidences in life. My parents' bond with the Ryersons juxtaposed with my sister preparing to leave the physical plane was pure Spirit in motion. The result of this bonding was the manifestation of a place the Touhey children could call home. What a gift!

My older sisters had a lot to do with enabling us to stay in the house. They all worked so we could keep a roof over our heads. I am forever grateful to them for it and the measure of stability it gave our family. As a result, the six younger children were blessed with consistency they hadn't had up to this point in their lives.

I enrolled at Sacred Heart School in Dover for my second try at fifth grade. I'd been expelled from Immaculate Conception School in May of the previous school year (more about that later). It was already October now, so I was going to be the new kid again. When I walked into the class, Sister introduced me to the class and told me I could sit next to the other new boy, who had arrived weeks earlier. His name was Tony Cannon. I was grateful not to be the only newbie. What a godsend, I thought. I wondered if he was as scared as I was. Tony still lives in Dover and we're still friends. I see him occasionally when I visit my mother and sister.

Although I did feel some fear, my feelings were different with this move. I had an instinct that Dover was home. The stability of having one home for a period of years helped me recover from the traumatic experiences of living on Grove Street and Glen Ridge. I know now it was the soft hand of Regina on my heart providing this feeling of belonging and being at home.

There was a lot of healing going on for the next four years while I was a student at Sacred Heart School. I remained pretty cautious most of that first year. Then gradually the consistency of staying in one place began helping my soul to heal and my personality to flourish. Within a school community, I felt part of something bigger than myself. I started to meet more and more kids and extend myself a little more each year. I always held back a little and never got really close to any one student, but I had lots of friends. I kept my guard up a little because I didn't know with absolute certainty that this was permanent or if I would come home from school one day and find the house packed for yet another move. But my personality was emerging and I discovered that kids liked me and wanted to be around me.

6

The Miracle of Friendship

"TO THE SOUL, THERE IS HARDLY ANYTHING
MORE HEALING THAN FRIENDSHIP."
— *Thomas Moore*

As you already know, we moved many times when I was young. We usually moved at night with lights out in the moving van and no forwarding address. This wasn't anything like the moves that people in the military make in order to better serve the country or that upwardly mobile executives make to bigger houses. This was the "we're three months behind on the rent and the bills, let's get the hell out of Dodge" kind of move. Consequently, I learned not to invest too much time in developing friendships.

I was the new kid a lot and it embarrassed me. I used sports to prove my worth to all the kids. By the time we moved to Dover and I enrolled at Sacred Heart School, I'd already attended Sacred Heart School in Bloomfield, Immaculate Conception School in Montclair, Central School in Glen Ridge, River Styx School in Lake Hopatcong, St. Michael's School in Netcong, Mount Arlington School in Mount Arlington, and East Dover Elementary, for two weeks (phew!). Someone once asked me how long I attended St. Michael's and I responded, "Until the first recess, then we moved." That wasn't far from the truth!

Once we moved to Dover and I was in one school for a while, I began to feel comfortable. Although I really didn't have any close friends, I was very popular. By the time I was in eighth grade, I was voted class president.

After I graduated from eighth grade, it was a really frightening experience to start my high-school career at Dover Junior High. Most of the class from Sacred Heart went to Morris Catholic High School. But since I had failed the entrance exam I was going to Dover public schools. In retrospect I'm so grateful I did, because I met three men at Dover High School who were the basis for the Miracle of Friendship. Before we became friends I walked the halls scared to death and felt completely alone. Hanging out with some guys I knew from midget football and Little League baseball was my only other option. At least I had some company at lunchtime. The truth is that they didn't like me much, and the feeling was mutual. They often made fun of me because I was a skinny Sacred Heart kid with no money, ate peanut butter and jelly for lunch every day, and wore clothes that weren't making any fashion statements.

Someone I knew from Sacred Heart lived next door to David Loeb and introduced us. David introduced me to his childhood friend, Michael Gruber, and their friend, Danny Benz. They all played basketball. I had started playing more basketball in eighth grade and really loved the game. I wanted to get to know these guys better, but knew it was improbable if I didn't qualify for the basketball team.

Realistically, there was no reason to think I could make the freshman basketball team at DHS. Nevertheless, I had hope instilled in me by my sister that just maybe I could do it. Hope wasn't the same as confidence, and it wasn't a belief or a certainty in my mind. I loved basketball, but I was a terrible player at that time. It was going to take something special for me to make the team. And something special happened. Because of my hard work in the preseason, Coach Cagnasola didn't have the heart to cut me from the team. I don't think he was consciously aware of how much I needed to make the team, but he knew on some very deep level. My name was on the list of those who made the team. Wow!!

The Miracle of Friendship blessed me when I made the team. My friendships with Danny, Michael, and David altered my life. Having these three friends at this crucial period of development is truly a miracle to me. I have met many people and had many friendships over the years. But without Danny, Michael, and David I'm not sure

I would have been able to get through my teen years. The importance of these guys and their families is immeasurable. I know they love me. The depth of gratitude and love I feel for them, because they helped save my life, is so very deep it can be painful. They probably think we are just friends, not aware they are lifesavers. I owe them so much. They will always live in my heart.

My oldest daughter, Serena, listens to a lot of my music and watches concerts on DVD with me. Tears come to my eyes when I hear certain music, and she asks me what's wrong. I tell her nothing's wrong—my tears are happy, loving tears. The songs remind me of my three friends and what they meant to me at such a vulnerable time in my life.

> *Most people are not clear on what is truly important to them. Because almost every life decision is guided by our values, it is imperative to identify them.*

These friends' families meant the world to me. I felt such safety in their homes, unlike the hypervigilance I had to maintain in my own home. I have wonderful memories of Mrs. Gruber cooking steak and veggies for me in the kitchen of their home in Dover. It was a small thing to her, I'm sure, but it meant a lot to me. So many times in my home there was no food, virtually nothing to eat, sometimes for a week or more—if anything, maybe a raw potato or biscuits made from flour and water. The food I stole from stores and the school cafeteria was often all I had to eat. Mrs. Gruber seemed so happy to feed me, and I was overjoyed more than she could possibly know. For two or three years, we boys helped her open their summer house on Lake Hopatcong by cleaning windows. The payoff was always a great spaghetti dinner. It was wonderful to be able to relax, feel safe and be fed.

It's funny how everything is relative. I talked to Kathy Gruber at Michael's fiftieth birthday party and told her how much I enjoyed her mother's cooking. She rolled her eyes and said her mom was a terrible cook, while I thought I was in culinary heaven! Mrs. Gruber often commented that she knew the Touhey boys would not get out of line because our dad would not tolerate it. She always said it in a kidding way. As I was annihilating whatever food was in front of me, I thought, "If you only knew the level of violence in my house, you wouldn't kid about it." Since abused children are masters at hiding their pain and their family secret, she wasn't able to figure that out.

I loved going to the Loebs' house, too. Mr. Loeb was crazy about sports and it was a treat to hang out in their family room, watch a little of his beloved Knicks, and hear him analyze the game. Mrs. Loeb always asked about everyone, was always so glad to see me, and always had some tale to tell. This home was another very safe place to be. Mrs. Loeb was a teacher at DHS so it was terrific to see her in the halls (though I think a friend and I once locked her out of a classroom). In the spring and sometimes in summer I walked from my house to David's and shot baskets in his driveway. This ritual lasted well into our college years, but it's those days in high school I remember most. We would just hang out, talk, and shoot baskets. These weren't really games; there was no keeping score, just buddies hanging out in friendship.

I think what I loved then and still love about David is his gentleness. Even as a teen, David had a peaceful nature. With all the pain, fear, and rage I had bottled up inside, a heavy burden was lifted when I experienced Dave's energy. He probably thinks I just liked the great parties at his house, but it was so much more. I can hardly express how Dave, being so kind and solid, was an anchor for me. I didn't always act accordingly, but I am so glad he was such a big part of my life. Dave seemed to always have things in perspective regarding sports and his career. He had a good head on his shoulders and set a great example for me, which was such a gift. Today I admire the way he operates his dental practice. He seems to have the perfect blend of work and recreation while attending to the joys in his life and being financially prosperous. I am sure David didn't understand he was giving me that lesson. I wasn't always aware I was learning that lesson. All I knew was I wanted him to be my friend and I wanted to be around him.

I was so driven to be good in basketball that I am sure it made Dave uncomfortable. Danny was driven to be good, too, but the difference was the energy I'd created around training and playing the game. My life depended on me succeeding in sports. I had an almost unnatural urgency to make it big. I absolutely had to make it and be the best, always number one. My well-being, my peace, and the badge of success for our family were based on athletic success. So much depended on me being a great player. It was a real burden for a young man to carry. I am just glad that the miracle of Dave happened to me. I still love to go and visit Mrs. Loeb. As I sit in her family room I can feel the same safety, calm, and love I always enjoyed as a young man.

I want Dave to know that I held on to our friendship for dear life. I did-n't even let my paranoid father intimidate me into severing this friendship or my ties with Mike and Danny. My father had taught me that the object in any competitive endeavor was to win at all costs and not worry about anyone else. He established that credo for the boys in the family even in competing with one another and our friends. Fellowship, having good relationships, and caring about your teammates were secondary to making sure to win and get all the accolades. Despite that, I knew that I craved a lasting relationship with David, and that jealousy wasn't the desired outcome of being on a team.

We didn't lack a competitive edge with each other, but we always respected and honored our true friendship. My father made those friendships hard to keep because he wanted me to feel no one should get in the way of me being number one. I am proud of the fact that I stood up in the face of his pressure and made competing with my friends less important than our relationships.

> *Your personal power, self-esteem, and ability to build a strong personal foundation are derived from having your life values and life actions in alignment.*

In 1969, my senior year, we opened the season against Morristown High School, a major rival. The gym was packed and we had five senior starters: Danny, still my best friend all these years later, Mike, David, me, and Bobby McElwaine. It was a great game and we won in front of the home crowd, 53–50. Danny and David were the leading scorers and I had fifteen rebounds against a very tall opponent.

My father was beside himself with anger. "How could you let a stiff like Loeb outscore you?" he hissed. I can recall the conversation as if it was yesterday. "You'd better do more shooting if you want to be the star." I replied, "Dad, I had fifteen rebounds and shot the ball when I was open. It was a great game and we won." He muttered under his breath something about me being a sissy. His parting shot was, "Do you think Benz and Loeb care about you?" I thought to myself, of course they care about me, we're friends. What they care about is that we won. We were five friends winning a big game together. I was so glad I had managed to beat a good team like Morristown with the best friends I had in the world. My feelings were so intense; I felt that Dad was going to have to kill me to keep me away from these guys.

I recall another incident that really set my father off. We were undefeated, winning our first six games going into the big Christmas tournament at Morris Hills High School. Our first opponent was Parsippany. They had a good team and one great player in Jim Healy. We lost in triple overtime. I played a very average game. Had I played better we would have won. But David played well that night.

The next night we beat a bad Hanover Park team. I played well and Dave had another good game. I was voted onto the all-tournament team, though I really didn't deserve it; David did. I was embarrassed walking across the court to get the trophy. When I got home I told my dad, "Dave should have made the all-tourney team, not me." He told me never to say something like that again. He called me a loser and asked me if I thought Loeb would give a crap if the situation were reversed. He kept at it, pounding me with his theme of not trusting anyone, even those I thought were my friends. But I knew with every fiber of my being how much I loved the guys and I knew I would not let go of my bond with them. Standing up to my father in that situation has always made me very proud.

Mike lived right around the corner from me, but I didn't know him until ninth grade, when we played basketball. I spent a lot of time at Mike's house. In our freshman year I walked to his house and picked him up on the way down the hill to meet Danny and David. Then we walked to the junior high school together.

Mike and I always talked a lot before we got to the bottom of the hill. His family was rich by any standard I knew. He lived in a big house in Dover, full of nice things, and his family also had the house at the lake in the summer. I thought he lived like a king.

What I know in my heart about Mike was that he always made sure I was included and that I did not feel left out. I think the greatest example of that is an incident in our freshman year that I will never forget. As freshmen, the four of us sometimes went across the street from the junior high to Dick's Bakery after basketball practice. The first time we went there to buy donuts, I was embarrassed and made up some excuse about leaving my money at home. It must have been obvious to Mike that there was no money at home. Without fanfare he bought the donut for me. After that first time I never had to worry about being embarrassed again. He always made sure, in a very quiet way, that I had a donut with the rest of the guys.

> *When you identify your core values and begin to live by them, you can reach the deepest level of personal fulfillment.*

I am sure Mike doesn't even remember those acts of kindness; he's simply a kind and generous person. Like Dave, Mike is now a dentist, and he is still showing the Touheys his generous nature by working on my sisters' and mother's teeth at a reduced rate.

I loved playing basketball with Mike Gruber and watching him and Danny play. Mike had such confidence in his ability; he was a natural leader without really saying much. His attitude of calm and confidence was something that I admired tremendously. He had such a positive effect on me as a player and I was always attracted to the understated way he competed. I loved to watch him eat up the upperclassmen in practice when he was just a sophomore. He dressed for all the varsity games, so I looked up to him. In our sophomore year I was fighting just to start on the J.V. team, hoping to reach the level of Mike and Danny.

I want Mike to know that his injury in our senior year that ended his season had such a profound effect on me, it's nearly indescribable. It was devastating to me, and at the same time it taught me a lesson that I've drawn upon so many times in my life. To thank him is not nearly enough.

Often, when we all get together, we talk about how good we would have been if Mike didn't get hurt. My God, that is so true. We finished the season at 15–9, but we would have been fighting for the conference and county championships if Mike had played. The gift he gave me was the grace he showed in the face of losing his senior year of basketball. Basketball was important to Mike. Without a doubt, it was just as important to him as it was to Danny and me. He showed me that you can lose something very important to you and still exhibit courage and grace. Although I have never asked him, I often wondered how he could take that setback without going nuts. I wouldn't have had the courage that Mike had to manage life if it had been me. I believed that my father would have disowned me if I got hurt like that.

Mike demonstrated by his actions that there was life without basketball. At that point in my life, I didn't think there was anything as important as the game. Although I continued to believe that for many more years, Mike's example in that situation helped me when I eventually did walk away from the game at the supposed peak of my coaching career.

I know that if Mike hadn't gotten hurt, I would have been an even better player myself. Danny and I had a magic together when we played, but Mike was able to settle me down. He had a subtle ability to help me keep things in perspective. I had a great senior year anyway, but I sorely missed him as my teammate.

At basketball camp one year, Danny and Mike played in a late-night pickup game against some very good college players. We were between our junior and senior years. I had gone to the restroom, so I missed the chance to get in the game. I was so proud of the way Mike ran the show and had such confidence. Although I had finished my junior year as a top player along with Mike and Danny, I don't think I would have played as well as they did against the college guys. But I was so proud of how Mike and Danny played.

My low self-esteem told me that maybe I didn't deserve to be on the court—I wasn't worthy enough. I was carrying the shame of being a poor, abused little boy disguised as a basketball player. I was sad that I felt that way.

I loved being around Mike. He had a hoop made from a hanger, with shoelaces for the net, perched on top of his bedroom closet door. We played horse with a rolled up sock. He had perfected an endless number of shots from practicing there all the time. He just couldn't be beat at that game. We laughed out loud, it was such great fun. Just as I did at David's house, I relaxed a little and enjoyed myself at Mike's.

I recall playing a game against Newton High School in my senior year. Mike was already hurt so he skipped the game to scout an upcoming opponent. I remember the bus pulling in and seeing Mike walking toward the bus to greet us, his scouting report in hand. My eyes teared up; I still couldn't believe that this great guy I loved was unable to play. I also thought that Mike's calm ability to lead would have helped in that Newton game, which we lost. I felt sad for him, for myself, and for the team. It occurred to me in that moment that as good as Danny and I were, we were not going to reach our goals without Mike. I also realized that this sad little boy inside of me was losing the steadying force in his life as a basketball player. I lost my teammate and the presence of the friend who always made sure I got a donut after practice.

My most profound relationship in all of my sports life was with Danny Benz. He was already a star in Dover when I met him. He was the leading scorer on the freshman team and I had barely made the cut. Even though my father truly loved Danny, he saw him as my competitor. But I saw him as an inspiration and set a goal to one day be as good a player as he. I did accomplish that feat—we were both named MVP of the team in our senior year.

I had so many experiences with Danny that it would take another book to write about all of them. Lacking that, I'll share as much as possible about the extraordinary friendship we had that sprang from our love of basketball. When I was with Danny, I really connected with how much I loved basketball in general and competition specifically. Danny and I played the game of basketball endlessly for the sheer joy of it. We didn't lack the competitive fire by any stretch of the imagination, but our pure love of the spirit of sport transcended competition and enriched our experience immeasurably.

We grew up playing pickup games in south Dover. We had no parents or coaches setting up the games, just a bunch of guys splitting up into teams and playing night after night. Danny and I always played on the same team and we rarely lost. We practiced and played so much, our game improved more than anyone's. We did it for ourselves and to contribute to Dover High School's great basketball team.

Danny and I played wherever we could. On Saturdays, we broke into the synagogue where Michael and David were members, since they had a small gym in the basement. As good Catholic boys, we had no idea that the Jewish Sabbath celebration occurred on Saturday, not Sunday. One cold March day, when the NCAA basketball tournament was being played, we picked teams to be and played games to ten points. We played the whole tourney one on one. All the commotion going on upstairs didn't bother us, but apparently the NCAA tourney did bother the worshipers. The rabbi was headed down the stairs. I said, "Hey, Danny, someone's coming, let's hide." Danny responded, "Quick, Kev, jump up on the stage and hide behind the curtains." We laughed hysterically as the rabbi looked around to find out who had been making that racket. We even forgave the rabbi for interrupting the greatest tournament on earth!

In those games of one-on-one, we competed against each other fiercely, as if we were playing against our biggest rival. But after the game, the admiration we had for each other was the real winner. While my father was preaching, "Look out for yourself, always make sure you know who your friends are, no one but family is really a friend," Danny taught me a different lesson.

When I made the team as a freshman, I was not a very good player, and spent most of the season watching my friends play from the bench. However, as the season went on I was getting better. Then came our game against Morris Catholic. I hadn't started a game yet, nor had I played very much at all. I watched from the end of the bench. Something was about to happen that would show me what real friendship is about. The Miracle of Hope provided by Regina Touhey was ready to sink its roots deeper and deeper into my soul.

I can't remember if Coach Cag told me in advance that I was starting in the game instead of Roy Curnow. I was amazed when he told me to go out and represent the team as captain with Danny before the game. I was so proud to be standing next to Danny as a captain in this special game. My sisters went to Morris Catholic. As a boy I had watched games in that gym, not Dover's. I had gone to countless football games at Morris Catholic and attended every play and Christmas show Maureen and Eileen starred in. Plus, almost every former classmate of mine from my eighth-grade class at Sacred Heart went to Morris Catholic and was in the stands to watch the game. And there I was, game captain with my best friend, Danny. I remember not listening at all to the pregame instructions from the referee, but just looking around the gym trying to make eye contact with everyone I had known from eighth grade. I was representing Dover High School's freshman basketball team out there in the middle of the court.

I had a great game. Danny was high scorer, but I think I scored eleven points. After the game, the Miracle of Danny Benz taught me something. I remember like it was yesterday. We were walking down the sidewalk from the gym to the bus and Danny said, "Wow, Kev, what a great game you played." He told me how happy he was for me. "You were the star today, Touhey," he continued. Here was a guy that was an all-star, yet he was happier for me than I had ever seen him be for himself. It wasn't just that I played well and we won. The moment was so much deeper than that. In that moment I knew that our friendship was so very important to him, that he cared for me and was happy for me. He certainly wasn't the competition to be feared or the rival who would keep me from getting my due. That moment gave me hope that I was worthy of a true friend who cared for me. I was right about what friendship could be and the joy it brought to the soul. I had a warm, rich feeling inside. I have loved Danny very deeply ever since.

There is a tremendous power in living your life by your highest ideals. Inner peace, long-range happiness, and a sense of certain direction are all results of knowing what is important in your life.

In the years to come I drew on that lesson time and time again. I got better and better as a player, and with that came more pressure from my father. There was a tough road ahead for me in basketball at Dover High, but the hope from the game at Morris Catholic and my relationship with The Benzer carried me through. From then on, I knew that the best basketball player in Dover cared about my success. He taught me we could compete with each other, push each other, and still share the limelight—and, most importantly, share a bond of friendship.

The times between the games and the seasons were where the relationship continued to grow. Shooting baskets on the playground together played a big part in that growth. I could just have fun loving the game. I didn't have to worry about my father looking over my shoulder.

After we left the synagogue on Saturdays, we went to Danny's house next door. We cooked hot dogs and ate a bunch of them. We talked about how good the team was going to be and our aspirations for ourselves. I think those moments are where the foundation for real friendship was laid.

Danny and I had a million moments of playing basketball over a period of about twenty years. We played on courts and in gyms all over North Jersey, from playground hoops to high school to adult leagues. We won a lot. The good times after those playing experiences were just as important as the games. We graduated from making hot dogs to eating at Travelers Diner in Dover after high school games, then drinking beer after our adult-league games. We played with a lot of different players in those various venues. The one constant was our bond of friendship. We were, and still are, connected in a way that is extraordinary.

Mr. and Mrs. Benz were like second parents to me. They supported me in a powerful way. I could really feel their love, and it was a major source of comfort. Mr. Benz used to take us to Travelers Diner after games and treat us to huge bowls of spaghetti. That was great. They were great to all of the Touhey boys.

LESSON 5

VALUES: THE KEY TO PERSONAL EMPOWERMENT

Most people travel through their lives unaware of the forces that guide them. They never sit in silence and identify what is truly important to them. They spend a lifetime making decisions and reacting to the stimuli of the world without soulful reflection.

The goal of this exercise is to truly identify your core values. When you are aware of your values and live by them, you are living a life filled with integrity. Knowing your core values provides a powerful force guiding the direction you take in life. If you are not in touch with your true values, it is difficult to maintain self-esteem and find long-term happiness.

Living your values creates personal power. Having a philosophy and taking actions based on this philosophy provides you with a sense of certainty, an inner peace, and a powerful inner strength. It is important that you set goals that are reflective of your true values. If you are setting and achieving goals that are not based on what you really want to accomplish in life, you may feel unfulfilled.

Sometimes your values conflict or are incompatible, so it is important to have a ranking system. This hierarchy of your values is best arrived at on the heart level. You'll make an investment of time and energy to evaluate your values and align your actions appropriately.

It is important to distinguish between "ends" and "means" values. I call this the difference between success and excellence. Success is the outward trappings that are obtained by striving to get them. It is a tangible measurement of results based on the actions you have taken. Excellence is more about the inner workings of your spirit as you travel on the road toward the successful outcome. It is the process or journey of getting there.

Excellence is about the day-to-day, minute-to-minute passion of your life's direction. The end result of a journey full of values based on excellence will reflect love, contribution, peace, and serenity. These attributes will provide the basis for true joy while you travel on the road to success. Money, success, career, and all the other tangible benefits have a deeper meaning when you are attached to excellence.

True value clarification makes your actions more meaningful and rewarding. True fulfillment and enrichment comes with your right actions based on excellence values. It is common for people to achieve their "success" goals and then wonder, "Is this it? Is this all there is?"

Exercise 5

VALUES CLARIFICATION

1. What are the most important things in your life? What do you value?

_____

_____

_____

_____

_____

2. In what ways is your decision-making process affected by your values?

_____

_____

_____

_____

_____

3. What do you think your values would need to be in order to create the personal empowerment you need to reach your ultimate goals in life?

_____

_____

_____

_____

_____

4. What are some of your present values that you need to release in order to reach your ultimate goals? How have these values held you back?

_____

_____

_____

_____

_____

5. What values might you need to add in order to achieve the life you truly want to have?

_____

_____

_____

_____

_____

6. What values do you have that present a challenge because they may be incompatible?

_____

_____

_____

_____

7. Whom do you admire and what values do they exemplify?

_____

_____

_____

_____

WHAT'S YOUR STORY?

Please journal about your own values. Do you live by them? How would your life be better if you had a clearer view of what is important to you?

_____

_____

_____

_____

_____

PART
3
CONSISTENCY

"PART OF COURAGE IS SIMPLE CONSISTENCY."
— *Peggy Noonan*

Children need consistent behavior from their caregivers. On a scale of 1 to 10, I was a 1. There was no consistent behavior present in my childhood at all. I lived my life in a state of hypervigilance, never knowing what the next crisis was going to be.

My mom told me that my dad held over fifty different jobs during his lifetime. Taking into consideration that he was a police officer for five years and worked at the County College of Morris in Randolph, New Jersey, for thirteen years, he held numerous other jobs in a very short period of time. My dad rarely worked a job for more than a few months before he quit or got fired. In 1970 he got the job at CCM because I played basketball there. I left home in 1973. In the time I lived in the Touhey household, he was usually moving from job to job or unemployed. In fact, for three of my high-school years he was basically unemployed.

In addition, before we moved to Dover I had attended seven schools and lived in seven different homes. The not knowing what was going to happen next provided the backdrop of inconsistent living—an early life of living in quicksand, waiting to be pulled out.

7

The Touhey Family on the Move

"THE LACK OF EMOTIONAL SECURITY OF
OUR AMERICAN YOUNG PEOPLE IS DUE, I
BELIEVE, TO THEIR ISOLATION FROM THE
LARGER FAMILY UNIT. NO TWO PEOPLE—NO
MERE FATHER AND MOTHER—AS I HAVE
OFTEN SAID, ARE ENOUGH TO PROVIDE
EMOTIONAL SECURITY FOR A CHILD. HE
NEEDS TO FEEL HIMSELF ONE IN A WORLD
OF KINFOLK, PERSONS OF VARIETY IN AGE
AND TEMPERAMENT, AND YET ALLIED TO
HIMSELF BY AN INDISSOLUBLE BOND WHICH
HE CANNOT BREAK IF HE COULD, FOR
NATURE HAS WELDED HIM INTO IT BEFORE
HE WAS BORN."

— *Pearl S. Buck*

Our eviction from our home in Bloomfield, when I was eight years old, and the subsequent move to Lake Hopatcong were very traumatic for me. I felt as though I was being ripped out of the womb. Not only were we moving our physical location and entering a period when we didn't have enough to eat and lacked the basics of life, but our entire way of life was altered. I think we all paid a price. For me, the little kid who loved his cousins and being near them, it was a terrible, isolating separation. I was going from the safety of the extended family into the unknown. When we drove to Bloomfield to visit my aunts and cousins, it felt like such a long ride from Lake Hopatcong and everything else that was at the root of our existence.

My father had sold a car to a woman who owned some houses on Lake Hopatcong. We used to go there for family outings when we lived in Bloomfield, so my parents were familiar with the area. But right when our financial situation was taking a turn for the worse, the safety net of being near extended family was eliminated. That feeling of belonging, the one human need that was actually being satisfied in my life, was about to cease. We were going to move to the "country," removed from everyone and everything familiar. People in Essex County went to Lake Hopatcong for vacation, not to live. The next four or five years were going to be very difficult. The groundwork for the feeling of severe instability was laid with this first move to the lake, speeding our downward spiral into economic disaster and abject poverty. Until we moved back to Essex County three years later, I felt like a fish out of water.

Once we moved to Lake Hopatcong, we did not see much of my cousins. One summer, the Carters rented a house on the lake for a week. I was very excited that they would be nearby and we visited and went swimming together. It was great to see them again. Another time they came to the lake and all of us—Joe and Robbie and the six Touhey kids—went into the woods to play in an abandoned house. Robbie hid in one of the many corners of the house and jumped out at Maureen as she came around the corner. He really scared her, and we all laughed out loud about it and carried on about the trick Robbie had played. It was such a great reminder of what it was like when we lived in Bloomfield, close to my cousins. That feeling of belonging to something bigger than us had returned, for a short while, anyway. We had our extended family once again and it was absolutely joyful!

8

The Miracle of Poverty

"POVERTY OFTEN DEPRIVES A MAN OF ALL
SPIRIT AND VIRTUE; IT IS HARD FOR AN
EMPTY BAG TO STAND UPRIGHT."
— *Benjamin Franklin*

In the early years of my life, I was not aware that we lived with so much financial strain. In retrospect, during my first six or seven years, there were indications of strain even though my dad was employed, first as a police officer and then as a car salesman. My sister Eileen asked me if I remembered pulling down signs that were posted on the telephone poles on Newark Avenue in Bloomfield announcing that the Touhey family was being evicted. I remembered taking down the signs, but I had forgotten the reason.

Our family grew quickly when Mom and Dad started having children. In rapid succession there was Kathleen, Maureen, Eileen, me, Brian, and Dennis. So even when my father was working, it must have been overwhelming just to feed the six of us.

The downward spiral started in earnest when a new ruling for police officers was put in place. All officers were required to take civil service tests, even if they had been on the force for a long time. My father did not even attempt to take the test. He had never finished high school and he lacked the self-confidence to try. My mother begged him to study, but he refused. In the end, he was released from the police force. However, he had some connections in the right places and he was placed in a job in the sheriff's department. He was guarding the jail. I remember him taking me to the jailhouse; I saw the men behind bars and I was scared. As it turned out, he just needed to lay low for a few years and he might have been able to get back on the force. But he hated the job and did not have the perseverance to wait it out. He quit, in spite of the fact that he had six mouths to feed. We would live in poverty for the remainder of my childhood.

> ## Attitude is crucial for creative problem-solving.

The reality of being so impoverished hit home when we moved from Bloomfield to Lake Hopatcong. Many families move and are just fine after an adjustment period. But the timing of our move was coupled with such financial instability that it magnified the pain that much more. I was becoming aware for the first time how little money we had. I was also becoming aware of the shame that can accompany poverty. The landlord always seemed to be showing up at the door asking for the rent. If my brothers and I were playing in the field across from the house, she stopped us and told us in a harsh tone to make sure our mother or father got in touch with her.

Eventually my mother went to work for the landlord in the flower business she owned and operated from a workshop in her basement. She had a huge house that sat on top of the hill, overlooking seven or eight other houses she owned. My mother's time in the shop didn't earn a paycheck. Her hourly wages were deducted from the back rent we owed. As a little boy, I climbed up the hill to visit my mom while she worked.

About seven years ago I took my wife and my mom back to take a look at the old house. It was burned out except for the beautiful stone foundation and chimney. The entire site was overgrown with thick brush. I was amazed to see my seventy-eight-year-old mother fight through the brush so she could get closer to the place where she once toiled for rent money. I always knew my mother had tremendous strength. That day, as I watched her determination to fight through that thick brush, I felt a new appreciation for the determination she possessed to make sure her family had a roof overhead. She fought through the brush with the same will that took her up that hill forty years earlier to work for the landlord. I am so grateful she had the will to keep the family together while my father struggled with all his demons.

There were indications the Touhey family was headed for even tougher times. We would live a nomadic existence for the next three or four years. My dear sister Regina was born and died during this time. We moved from Bloomfield to Lake Hopatcong, and the owner eventually evicted us from that house too. I went to St. Michael's and River Styx School while living in Hopatcong. The next couple of years found all us kids attending numerous schools.

Once, when our electricity had been cut off, my cousin Tom and his family came to visit. I will never forget the scene—candles all over the place to illuminate the house. My mother made some excuse about why we had no lights.I remember Tom thought it was cool.He said,"Hey,guys, this is what it must have been like during the Civil War days! Isn't this great?" I said to myself, "Cousin, I'll trade you. I will trade you all the candles and hunger at my house for lights and food at yours. What do you say?"

I felt my mother's shame as she made up some story to explain to her sister the reason we were all sitting around in the dark. My mom had a lot of pride and I know it really hurt her to think her sister suspected anything about our financial troubles. Over the years, I heard my mom telling many stories to many people to keep our shameful existence a secret. A good story could deflect some of the truth of this utter poverty that was our life.

Over the years I learned that I too could pretend to others that everything was really all right. Even though I was embarrassed and ashamed on the inside, I didn't have to let the outside world know that. I learned to act as if all was just dandy in the Touhey household. But I also held onto that little bit of hope through all of the turmoil. I had a little voice inside saying hang in there; good times, food, electricity, and harmony in the family are right around the bend.

My beliefs and perceptions about lack in my life were etching their way into my being. These feelings were a tremendous challenge to the hopeful feelings that also resided there. I was a battleground for a schizophrenic war between knowing everything was going to be all right and feeling that we were going down the tubes. Sometimes the shame and poverty felt overwhelming. At the same time, I believed that if I just hung in there my father would find that one job that would provide us with the safety and consistency that all children need. The only problem is, our brains can't hold two conflicting thoughts at the same time, so the dichotomy was hugely unsettling.

When the owner finally had enough of our nonpayment of the rent, we were evicted and moved across the lake to Mount Arlington. We were enrolled at the Mount Arlington School. Since our move from Newark Avenue in Bloomfield just a year earlier, I was now entering my third school in a year. And during our stay in Mount Arlington, our poverty was magnified into a pain so deep it changed my enthusiasm for life. Until this point, I had never experienced this total heavy darkness that was now being etched in my soul. I felt poor, very poor, and I felt all the shame that comes with living in poverty. What's worse, it was in Mount Arlington that Regina got sick and died. That made the situation in the Touhey family almost unbearable for this little boy. It took a lot of holding onto hope to get through this time.

9

The Miracle of Begging

"AS FOR BEGGING, IT IS SAFER TO BEG THAN
TO TAKE, BUT IT IS FINER TO TAKE THAN TO
BEG."

— *Oscar Wilde*

I had to beg for food for the first time in Mount Arlington. Down the street from our house, there was a grocery store and bar owned by a pair of Italian brothers. My father sometimes drank at the bar when he had money.

One day I was in the kitchen and my mother asked me if I would go to the store and ask the grocer to give us some hot dogs on credit. It must have been very painful for my mother to ask her eight-year-old son to go and plead for food. But she was a survivor, and whatever it took to get food on the table was what had to be done. I think my mom knew an eight-year-old with an empty belly and many hungry siblings would have better luck than she.

I went to the store with confidence. Surely this man would understand that we needed food. We had a very sick little girl in the house, and how could he want her to go without food?

What followed was a humiliating experience. I was about to learn about "The Book" for the first time.

The store owner produced the book he kept for people who bought food on credit. The Touhey family had charged an extensive list of items but hadn't paid yet. He sternly said to tell my parents there was no room in the little book to charge more food. He also told me to tell my dad to get a job and pay off all the items we had already gotten. Despite all that, he gave the hot dogs to me! To this day I remember how wonderful those hot dogs tasted! I felt embarrassed and ashamed, but we had some great spicy store-made franks that day.

> *Handling problems in a simple, systematic way is very powerful and satisfying.*

My family had no money and my father wasn't working. The gnawing feeling in the pit of my stomach was more than not having enough to eat; it was the shame of this state of lack. It felt demeaning to have someone else hold power over me, especially to decide whether or not I was worthy enough to merit food.

I vowed that when I got older, I would never ask anyone for anything. I was determined to make sure I'd never feel that humiliation again. As a result, when I did have to ask for help, it was very painful. The deep embarrassment I felt when I needed assistance as an adult had its roots in places like that little local grocery store.

What I learned had both positive and negative effects. I decided at a very young age that I alone would be responsible for my own welfare, no matter what the circumstances. Unfortunately, I learned the hard way that it's embarrassing to ask anyone for even legitimate help when you need it. My unwillingness to have others help or assist me in any way often did me harm.

My belief about asking for help was cemented on January 19, 1961, one day before the inauguration of JFK. Regina was in the hospital; she would die two days later. A tremendous snowstorm raged outside and tremendous hunger and anger raged inside the house on Howard Boulevard in Mtount Arlington, New Jersey. I was nine years old, Brian was six, and Dennis was five. Mom told me that that we needed some food. I was aware the grocer across the street wouldn't help since we had outstanding debt in that little book he kept.

My mom said I would have to try another store a mile up the road. I asked my mom if *they* had one of those books that said we were poor and owed a lot of money, but she said that we didn't use the store often so we should be okay.

Mom told me to take my brothers with me because my father was upstairs ranting, raving, and crying. She thought it would be best for all of us to get out of the house. I am sure he was feeling shameful about having no job, no food for his family, no means of transportation, and worst of all, no hope. His own grief drove him mad.

There were eight starving children and two starving adults in the house. It was up to this little band of brothers to go out and rescue the Touhey family.

Mom bundled us up the best she could. We had no gloves and it was very cold, so she told us to keep our hands in our pockets as much as possible. Brian and I teamed up to take care of Dennis. My mother sent us all off with a kiss and a look of terror on her face.

We had a sled and pulled Dennis on it most of the two miles. Sometimes we pulled together; sometimes we switched to take turns keeping our hands in our pockets. It took us a long time to get to the store. The whole way I was planning what to say when we arrived there. I felt a heavy weight of responsibility: I had to get food for the family, no matter what it took. I was going to convince this man that he had to help us.

At first Brian and I were chugging along, pulling Dennis as fast as we could. We made a game out of it, trying to make some sort of fun out of a very hard experience. But our hands began to get colder and colder. The sled got heavy, as though we were pulling a truck. We were small, the road was long, and the fun and games had turned to drudgery. We were merely surviving. We stopped talking and put our heads down and trudged through the snow to get some food. We thought only of securing a meal for our family.

I can see the owner as clearly as if this all happened yesterday, not forty-five years ago. I said to him, "We have walked all the way from home in the snow, sir, it's a long way and we're freezing. My family has no car, my dad has no job, and all my brothers and sisters are really, really hungry. Would you give us some food?" It was the truth and he would surely understand our dilemma.

He looked at me with pure pity. But he responded, "There's no way I can give you any food, son."

My little heart sank. I protested, but he told me, "This is how I make a living; working in this grocery store is how I feed my family. Maybe your father should get a job so he can feed you." I told him my dad was real sad because my sister Regina was dying. He said he was sorry about that, but he could not give us any food. With that, Brian looked terribly sad and forlorn. Dennis was just shivering and trying to warm up. I said "Please" one more time. With a sad look on his face the owner told me, "You'd better leave the store and take your brothers home, son."

I had failed my family. It was my responsibility to get food for us all. The shame of failure ran deep and I dreaded going home.

We began our journey back home, silent all the way. It was snowing harder now, and I felt defeated.

My mind swirled with questions. Why couldn't my dad get a job like other dads? Why did I have to go ask for food? Why were my brothers and I out in this storm trying to get home, and with no food? What would happen when we got there?

The uncertainty of all this was more than a nine-year-old boy could endure. The hardship of that day gave birth to a little adult Kevin, as though I'd grown up all at once. Things were different from then on.

As the oldest, the one in charge, I needed to be strong. I told Brian, "We're going to take turns pulling Dennis." I told Dennis, "You're going to have to walk some, little brother." I wanted him to walk a little at a time so Brian and I could have a break from pulling all the weight. I told them both that we were going to be all right and make it home.

They were troupers, both as strong in their resolve as I. There were no tears or complaining. I can see little Denny getting off the sled to do his share, his little legs carrying him through the piles of snow. Brian, with his physical strength and mental resolve, took his turn pulling the sled. We were three amigos bound together by a bountiful love for each other, trudging home without the bounty.

Perceived problems are the road to opportunity and success if properly handled.

When we got home my mother was waiting at the door. I saw the concern on her face. She took care of us right away and told me it was all right that we were unable to talk the grocer into giving us food. After she took care of my brothers she looked at my hands and told me, "Go to the bathroom, Kevin, so I can warm your hands." I started to cry.

I cried because my hands hurt from the cold. I cried from total exhaustion and being soaking wet from head to toe. I cried from relief that my brothers and I had made it home safely. But mostly I cried because I didn't get food for my family.

I still remember seeing my father lurking at the top of the steps. He did not come down to see if we were all right. Instead he bellowed, "Stop crying, you big baby." My mom said quietly to me, "Go sit and get warm, it will be all right."

The entire Touhey family went to bed hungry that night. And I felt guilty for failing them.

I believe my father was simply overwhelmed by our situation. I have such deep compassion for him. Though he wasn't truly helpless, I'm sure he felt that way. I think my father felt at his core that he was unworthy and had no talent. He didn't believe he had what it took to hoist himself out of the situation, never mind nine other family members. That must have been a very shameful place to inhabit every day; I know he felt a tremendous amount of shame.

My mom had to be strong in the face of all of this or the family would have fallen apart. She had to balance all the chaos of my father's life and take care of eight children too. It took faith and strength to manage all that. She had to be a rock and use any methods necessary to keep us all from drowning. I think in some ways she had to seal herself off emotionally to survive. That took a toll on us because it created an emotional disconnect with her. I know she loved us, but with all the drama and just plain surviving, there wasn't much time for bonding.

In the fall of 2006 I went back to that store to take pictures for this book. My daughter Serena went with me. The store still has the same name on the front, but it is a liquor store now. I started to talk to the man who was working in the store, the owner's son. I told him the story of the snowstorm. We talked for twenty minutes about a lot of things. His father had died recently. I loved the sense of continuity with the son following the father in the business. The encounter gave me a powerful feeling of déjà vu.

LESSON 6

CREATIVE PROBLEM-SOLVING

Problems arise because life moves pretty fast and has a thousand interruptions. It isn't always easy to solve problems without some basic skills of discernment. However, problems can be opportunities for personal growth. It is your awareness, your perception of the challenge, that is the key. In many cases, the feeling state you have attached to the problem presents more of a challenge than solving the problem. By adding significance to how you feel about the situation, your reaction sometimes makes the problem worse. When you combine positive thinking, creative enthusiasm, and optimism with the proper perspective, there are few challenges that you cannot resolve.

When you cultivate an attitude of turning every stumbling block into a stepping stone or making every breakdown an opportunity for a breakthrough, you learn that problems are temporary. Very few problems need to be permanent. Your own attitude will determine this.

Here's a great question to ask yourself when you perceive a challenging situation: "Can I really do anything about the problem?" Is it worth the effort or is it just an emotional reaction?

Exercise 6

MASTERING PROBLEM-SOLVING

1. List five situations, events, or concerns that you feel are problems in your life. Why do you consider them problems? What would it take to get them handled?

_____

_____

_____

_____

_____

2. Describe your attitude toward the problems in your life.

_____

_____

_____

_____

_____

3. Are you responsible for any of your problems? How so?

_____

_____

_____

_____

_____

4. Do you think you have the power or ability inside you to creatively solve all the problems that come your way? If so, describe this power. If not, why not?

_____

_____

_____

_____

_____

5. Why do you think that some people are able to overcome their problems while others are overwhelmed by theirs?

_____

_____

_____

_____

_____

WHAT'S YOUR STORY?

Please journal about any thoughts on problems that you may have come to in reading the chapters and doing the exercises so far.

_____

_____

_____

_____

10

The Miracle of Surviving the Paint Can

"WE SHALL DRAW FROM THE HEART
OF SUFFERING ITSELF THE MEANS OF
INSPIRATION AND SURVIVAL."
— *Winston Churchill*

I'm not sure what I was thinking. How was I going to get away with this prank? It was certainly going to be a miracle if I pulled this off without some degree of retribution. It was way beyond optimistic to think there wouldn't be a high price for the actions I was about to take.

The fifth-grade class at Immaculate Conception School in Montclair, New Jersey, consisted of approximately fifty well-groomed, well-behaved students stuffed into one classroom. I don't think I knew even one student by name, but I didn't really care. I had loads of friends in the high school.

It was April, it was baseball season, it was nice outside, and I was bored to tears with all the schoolwork. I was failing every one of my subjects and report cards had come out six weeks earlier. We were supposed to have them signed and returned. Instead, mine was hidden very safely in a closet on the third floor of the home we rented in Glen Ridge, New Jersey. My mom and my sisters were in on the plot to keep this example of academic ineptitude from my dad. He hadn't been in very good shape since my sister died. He was drinking heavily and he would be furious if he saw my report card. There was no telling how long we could keep it from him, but we never discussed that.

I remember very vividly being in the kitchen with my mom and my three sisters as Kathy explained to him, "Yes, Dad, the high school always gets the report cards first."

My dad responded, "I don't remember you girls getting your reports earlier than Kevin last time."

My mother jumped in: "Oh yes, Jim, they did get them before Kevin came home with his. Why don't you call Joey, he'll tell you." Now it was a stroke of genius that my mom suggested that. My dad knew our cousin Joey would not lie, so the mere suggestion carried a lot of weight. It was pure genius because our phone was turned off. There was no way to contact Joey. My mom and sisters were utterly convincing.

But the action I was about to take was going to blow the cover off that well-conceived plot to save me from my father's vengeance!

Let's get back to the classroom where I sealed my fate. As I got out of my seat, which was actually obscured by a pillar, I got as low to the ground as possible and kept my eye on the cloakroom. As I crawled down the aisle, the students on either side looked at me with amusement and bewilderment on their faces. I did not have a clue what I was going to do once I reached safe haven, but it promised to break the boredom of Sister's intended lesson.

By the time I got to the Promised Land, about three-fourths of the class had noticed and were reluctantly giggling. They were probably not totally sure if giggling at such a foolhardy move constituted a sin or not. I imagine they were pretty confident that my aisle-crawling would merit at least an extended stay in purgatory, if not full-time burning in hell for eternity. They did not want to risk any sin by association.

As I stood up to take those last few steps into the cloakroom, Sister saw me. Adjusting her rosary beads so she wouldn't trip over them, she made a beeline after me. I quickly closed the cloakroom door and was relieved to see I could lock it from the inside. Sister would have to get the key to get me out.

I chuckled in delight as the class threw caution to the wind and started to roar in laughter at Sister's frustration. I guess they figured that maybe a quick confession with Father Glee would absolve them from the sin of laughing at the good sister. So they helped themselves to a hearty belly laugh until Sister twirled in a rage and told them they'd better be quiet or they would have enough homework to last well into their teens.

Then she turned her attention back to me and at the top of her God-given lungs she yelled, "What you are doing, Mr. Touhey, this will surely give God the rest of the evidence He needs to prove your unworthiness and send you straight to hell!" Whenever the good sister started a sen

tence with the formal version of my name, I knew I was in trouble. The old "Mr. Touhey" lead-in was an indication that what would follow was not going to be pleasant.

Resigned to my fate, I decided to go out in a blaze of glory by shooting not one but both middle fingers right up against the glass of the Promised Land's door into the red, yelling face pressed up against the window. An eerie quiet came over the room. Little did I know that in four short hours, I would be in hell right here on earth, in the garage of my home in Glen Ridge.

It had been a very hard year leading up to the cloakroom incident. The Touhey family had taken a huge blow when our beloved Regina died eighteen months earlier, alone in a hospital room at St. Claire's Hospital in Denville, New Jersey. My father was drinking heavily and hardly working. He was coaching football at Immaculate Conception High School, which was fun, but in spite of that, he was an angry man most of the time. I was about to be on the receiving end of fifteen months of pent-up frustration.

> *Know that you are not your boundaries and standards. You do not define yourself by them. They are merely tools.*

My descent into academic hell took place over time. Sometimes I left school and hung around until practice started. I never did my homework and I acted out in class in ways that weren't acceptable to the sister. I was caught throwing erasers at the cheerleaders from the second-floor window when I was supposed to be erasing the board as a punishment for something else I had done. Sister eventually had enough. She said, "Since you are acting like a second grader, I am going to put you in the second grade." Then I'd be in class with my good-as-gold brother Brian. "Maybe," Sister continued, "you can learn to behave if you're a few grades lower."

It was during basketball season, the day they put me in second grade with my brother. My cousin Joey yelled at me for the first time ever. I can still see him dribbling the ball across the court at the IC gym, and he was-n't smiling. He asked me, "What the hell are you doing getting thrown out of class? I don't want you here." He told me to leave practice and go home. I got some cigarettes from an older kid, went under a train trestle where I often hid to get away from the world, and smoked.

I didn't last long in second grade because I always told my brother the answers for his school projects. The sisters kicked me back up to fifth grade.

Now in the cloakroom, locked in with both middle fingers pressed against the glass, I suddenly realized that I was in real trouble. The feeling just washed over my entire being. I remember in great detail what followed. I unlocked the door, walked over to where my spring jacket was hanging, and waited for Sister to grab my ear and lead me to the principal's office. The principal of the school wrote a letter right there on the spot, telling my mom and my dad to accompany me back to school that night to discuss the repercussions of my actions. I am sure the nuns had to hold council to decide what the proper punishment should be for aisle-crawling, coupled with locking the sister out of the cloakroom and giving her my version of the "we're number 1" signal with both hands.

The first sentence of the principal's letter to my parents stated only that I was defiant and bold. It did not go into detail about what I had done. She thought I should be the one to tell my parents exactly what I'd done to deserve being characterized as defiant and bold. I was told to hand-deliver the letter to my parents. I knew I was in trouble and thought I would probably get a loud earful from my them, but I was way off in my assessment. Although I had witnessed the manifestations of my father's anger on other occasions, I had never seen this level of intense and utter rage.

You might ask where my parents were all this time. Were they not aware I was causing trouble? I think my mom knew part of what was going on, but not all of it. She knew I'd been put in the second grade with my brother. In an attempt to shield me from my father, she hadn't told him everything.

While I was writing this book, my sister Eileen told me that she was only now working on forgiving herself for not being able to help me with what happened next. She explained that her therapist was working with her through the guilt.

I gave the letter to my parents and watched as my dad read it. His rage distorted his handsome features. He put his finger in my face and yelled at the top of his lungs, "What did you do at school?" He shouted for me to tell him exactly what I had done, but I was unable to speak. The louder he yelled, the more I couldn't find my voice. At that point Eileen ran up to the third-floor bathroom and hid. It seemed as if anyone who could provide any help drifted away. Finally, in total frustration he screamed, "Get out to the garage right now. You just get out there and wait for me."

The walk to the garage seemed like an eternity and a millisecond simultaneously. I walked past the car in the driveway where, earlier that year, my dad and I had listened to the Liston-Patterson heavyweight championship fight on the car radio because we had no electricity in the house. It was fun and warm to share that with him. It was in these moments that the true nature of my father's soul was revealed. There was no anger, no struggle, in the purity of these moments with him. This was my father in pure spiritual form. There was only love for me as he held me tight to his side, the love a father connected to God has for his first-born son.

As I walked past the car this time, I knew that the end result of this outing would be anything but fun.

I stood in the garage and watched this six-foot-one, 220-pound man storm out of the house. Perhaps my mom had encouraged him to take it easy on me. As I watched him come toward the garage, I was reminded of a time when I was little and I stuck my hand in a fan. He slapped me real hard in the face for being a stupid three-year-old. I also vividly remembered the first time I saw him hit my mom. As these thoughts filled my mind, I got more and more frightened. I was not sure if I was going to be able to tell him what I had done at school that day. Then it occurred to me that I never remembered any family member being told to go somewhere outside the house to be punished. I knew it wasn't going to be pretty. I can't emphasize enough how terrified I was.

To this day I have no idea why I was unable to speak, but I just wouldn't tell him what I had done. I can see him warning me that I'd better tell him or he was going to give it to me good, which meant an awful beating. "What did you do?" he yelled. I just stared at him in fear. The words would not come.

I remember being determined not to cry. I couldn't stick to that. With the first blow I heard a crack as he hit me in the nose. I winced in pain and as the tears spurted out, so did a part of my spirit.

I looked him right in the eye as he delivered that blow. Again he bellowed to tell him what had happened. Blood flowed from my nose, but no words came out of my mouth. As he continued beating me, I screamed for help. My sister Eileen told me that those screams still haunt her today. Even while screaming, I decided that I was not going to allow him to knock me off my feet. With each blow my resolve to look him in the eye strengthened and he was unable to knock me down. That surely was a miracle, since I weighed about sixty-five pounds.

Before his final act of fury, he gave me one more chance to tell him what I had done. I opened my mouth but still the words just would not come. With my little fifth-grade body trembling, feeling like I might die if I did-n't find the words to tell my father what I'd done in school, I still could not speak.

Finally he backed away from me. I had stopped screaming now. The rage on his distorted face had not dissipated, but I felt some relief since he was backing away—until I saw him pick up a mostly empty paint can. As he spun around I spoke my first words of the entire ordeal: I yelled, "No, Dad, no," as he swung the paint can at the left side of my face. I cringed so the can hit my shoulder first and then crashed into my left ear. My shoulder took the brunt of that blow. I stopped crying. The beating was over.

> *Learn that creating standards and boundaries
> is an ongoing process and they can change as
> personal development takes place.*

Still in a rage, Dad told me to go inside to the bathroom and clean up my face. I remember walking back into the house and wondering where everyone was: Mom, three sisters, four brothers, where was everyone?

When I got to the second-floor bathroom and looked in the mirror, I felt so alone. I could not believe what was looking back at me in the mirror. What I saw was a very battered, bruised, scared, and sad little boy. For the first time since her death fifteen months earlier, I spoke Regina's name out loud. I simply said, "Regina, please help me."

As I cleaned my face, I was startled when the door was kicked open and there stood my father. He seemed even angrier than before. He came toward me and looked into my eyes and bellowed, "Are you going to tell me or do you want me to beat it out of you some more?" There was a strange calm in that moment as I finally whispered in a very small voice exactly what I had done at school that day. He changed in that moment, a remorseful look on his face, a trace of, "Oh my God, what did I do to this little boy of mine?"

I wasn't really aware of it then, but now I know my sister helped me to access my own soul and find the words. The spirit of Regina, called upon by a small prayer, filled the room with her calm presence. One could argue that the sight of my swollen face, with the bruising already discoloring it, was what startled my father out of his rage. I believe my small prayer asking Regina for help changed me so I could respond to his demand.

As I got dressed, I saw the first the first sign of another family member being present. My mother told me, "Hurry, Kevin, we don't want to be late getting to the convent." So I finished cleaning up and we were off for the scheduled visit with the nuns.

My mother did not hug me or hold me but I felt strangely strong. The ride in the car with my parents was strange, as if nothing out of the ordinary had just occurred. I remember actually leaning over the seat, talking to them. I don't remember what we were talking about. But it was a very calm ride to the convent.

> *Eventually your boundaries and standards become self-managing. They will become automatic.*

My mom kept saying over and over, "I just cannot believe that my good son Kevin could possibly have locked himself in the cloakroom and made an obscene gesture to the sister." She told the principal and my teacher that I was always helping her take care of my four younger brothers. Meanwhile, my father was assuring the sisters that I would make up for everything and become a shining example at the school.

I was sure that in spite of my terrible behavior at school that day and my failing every class, the nuns would feel sorry for me and reprimand my parents when they got a good look at my face. But that didn't happen.

I sat there in disbelief. There were four adults in the room with a very badly beaten little boy. The two nuns had just seen me five hours earlier. It didn't even occur to them to ask what happened to me between then and now—not even "Hey, Kevin, did you run into a truck on the way home?"

> *Understand that standards are about your behavior and boundaries are about the behavior of others.*

I knew right then and there that I was on my own. I would have to be careful about whom to trust. An incident like this chips away at a child's belief system. But I did not feel totally alone. On the ride home, I began to see that I could remain hopeful about myself and my ability to survive. I knew that with the spiritual support of my little sister, I had survived the onslaught of this very big man, my father. I thought that since I survived that, I could survive almost anything. Deep down I knew there was not going to be much that could keep me down.

Still, a part of me died in the garage that night. I left a piece of my heart on the floor with the blood and the paint can. I believe the spirit of my sister Regina picked it up and carried it around for the next twenty-nine years. It would take that long for me to come to grips with the pain of her death and the many volatile incidents that followed her passing.

As it turned out, the good sisters, dressed in their fine habits and rosaries, dripping with grace, mercy, compassion, and love, had told my father and mother that I was a delinquent not fit for the high moral standards upheld at Immaculate Conception. They expelled me and told me and my parents to take my battered body and soul to another school. But no other school would take me, so I stayed out altogether for a few months.

The next year I began fifth grade all over again at Central School in Glen Ridge. I hated it there. I felt out of place and ashamed. I was there only until October, when we moved to Dover and I enrolled at Sacred Heart School, my fifth school in two years. I was the new kid once again.

LESSON 7

CREATING HIGH PERSONAL STANDARDS AND BOUNDARIES

Although boundaries and standards are two separate items, they work hand in hand. Personal growth is really inhibited without high standards and strong boundaries. Boundaries protect you from certain behaviors of others. Standards are behaviors and actions to which you hold yourself.

It is important to understand that boundaries are a tool to keep people and situations at a reasonable distance emotionally so that they don't drain your energy. When you establish strong boundaries, fear diminishes and you are able to trust on a deeper level.

By setting boundaries you are training others in how you want to be treated. More often than not, these actions and attitudes increase the level of respect you get from others. By knowing what constitutes acceptable and unacceptable behavior toward you, others will naturally treat you with more respect. You can set boundaries with grace and gentleness. You should not set them with anger.

Setting high personal standards is a way of living that keeps you from living according to the whims, beliefs, and goals of others and of society. Standards are a statement about who you are and how you behave. For example, you are powerful, you are honest, and you accept others without judgments.

Exercise 7

SETTING YOUR STANDARDS AND ESTABLISHING BOUNDARIES

1. In what ways have you violated others' boundaries that you are aware of? Name three ways.

_____

_____

_____

_____

2. Identify what boundaries you currently have in place. What behaviors from others do you not allow?

_____

_____

_____

_____

3. Identify new boundaries you want to set. What five things will you no longer allow others to do around you, say around you, or expose you to?

_____

_____

_____

_____

_____

4. List three people you admire. What standards do they maintain that you could adopt?

_____

_____

_____

_____

_____

5. Have you ever used a standard of yours as a "holier than thou" judgment of others? Describe how.

_____

_____

_____

_____

_____

WHAT'S YOUR STORY?

Please journal about any new insights you've come to in this lesson. In what ways will you change how you treat people? In addition, what are you willing to change about yourself that will lead to a higher standard?

_____

_____

_____

_____

_____

_____

_____

_____

_____

_____

_____

_____

_____

_____

_____

My wife, Annabelle, on our front porch with our daughters. Serena is sitting right next to her and Ava is on the second step.

Ava and Serena strike a pose in the dining room.

I am standing next to the famous stone kneeler at St Mary's Hospital in Passaic, where my dad knelt and prayed for hours that a boy would be born into the Touhey family.

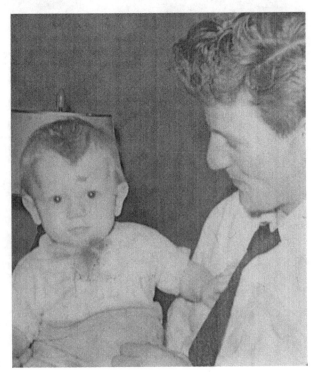

My dad holding me and showing me lots of love. This picture was taken while we lived in Nutley.

Dad leads the way as Mom carries me back from a dip in the ocean at Point Pleasant Beach in New Jersey. I learned early to love the water.

My sisters Eileen and Kathy (with our cousin, left) look on as Maureen tries to stop me from crying. This picture was taken behind my Grandmother Mimi's house one Easter Sunday in the early 1950s.

Dad posing in his police uniform, standing next to Mom in Mimi's backyard. That's me looking up at Dad with admiration.

(Clockwise from left) Dad, Maureen, me, Dennis, Brian, Regina. I am holding Regina upright for this picture taken on the side lawn of the Lake Hopatcong house in 1959.

Eileen holds Regina
in front of the house in Lake
Hopatcong, probably 1959.

My dear sister Regina in a
beautiful sundress in Lake
Hopatcong, 1959 or 1960.

The cousins taking a break from swimming at Lake Hopatcong. In the front row are *(left to right)* Eileen, Cousin Linda, a friend, and Maureen. In the back row are Cousin Tom, Brian, Dennis, and me.

Celebrating a family Thanksgiving in the early 1960s at our home in Dover. Sitting on the couch are *(left to right)* Cousin Tom, Brian, Dennis, and me.

Thanksgiving at our Dover home. Sitting on the couch *(left to right)* are Maureen, Cousin Linda, Eileen, and Kathy.

(Left to right) My mom, her Aunt Frya, Mimi (Mom's mother), and Mom's sister, Agnes, sitting at the dining-room table in Dover. This picture was taken at Thanksgiving in the early 1960s.

An early 1950s family picture with the Carter cousins and Grammy Touhey, Dad's mom. Kneeling in the front are Maureen and Eileen. Grammy Touhey has her arms around Joe, Rob, and Kathy. That's Mom holding me in the back.

Grammy Touhey surrounded by the family. First row, the boys (left to right): Brian, Dennis, me. Second row, the girls (left to right): Eileen, Maureen, Kathy holding Regina. Third row, Mom and Dad. This would have been taken in 1959 or 1960.

The Carter cousins at play with Eileen and Maureen up front and Cousin Robby, Cousin Joe, and Kathy clowning around in the back row.

A Touhey family picnic with Grammy Touhey in the early 1960s. That is Mom and Dad on one side of the table. The children, from front to back, are me, Dennis with his head sticking out, Brian, Kathy, Eileen, and Maureen.

This picture was taken the day of my First Communion in the living room of our home on Newark Avenue in Bloomfield. On the floor, in front, are Maureen and Eileen. On the couch are *(left to right)* Dad, Dennis, Cousin Rob, me, and Cousin Joe with Brian on his lap. Kathy is standing in the back.

The whole gang at a cookout at Eileen's house in 1985. Sitting on the first step *(left to right)* are Patrick, Tim, Maureen, and Cousin Beth. Sitting on the second step *(left to right)* are Cousin Joe, Eileen, Mike, and Kathy. Sitting on the third step *(left to right)* are Dad, Cousin Betty, and Cousin Rob. Standing at left are Cousin Tom, Cousin Linda, and Dennis. I am standing on the right.

I always loved this picture from the 1962 Immaculate Conception High School yearbook, because Dad and Joe are on the same page. That is Dad pictured with his freshman football team. He is standing on the far right. Right below the team picture, Cousin Joe gives some instructions to a player and coach.

I celebrate my election as eighth-grade president in 1965. You can see my slogan on the poster behind me: "Vote for Red and You Won't Be Blue."

Another post-election picture. It seems like I loved holding my campaign bear. I was probably seeking comfort from the wrath of Sister Eileen!

This is my freshman basketball team in 1966. It was a miracle I made the team! I am kneeling, second from the right.

Here I am in the summer of 1968 receiving my very first basketball trophy at the Camp of the Lakers in Honesdale, Pennsylvania. In the background are standing *(left to right)* Art Hyland and legendary coaches Butch van Breda Koff and Pete Carill.

Posing in the Dover High gym before our senior season, 1970. There is Benz in front and Loeb, me, and Gruber in back.

This picture was in the newspaper the day before the opening game of our senior year against Morristown High School. It appears that Danny and I did not know how to pass the ball out toward the camera so it would not cover our faces. Gruber was always the smart one.

That's me in my senior year, making a reverse lay-up against St. Bernard. I scored 23 points and had 7 rebounds to help us beat a very good opponent.

Backcourters 1990 Shine In Dover's Triumph

By LARRY SCHWARTZ

DOVER — Coach Pat Luciano probably has the best one-two scoring punch in the Lakeland area in Dan Benz and Kevin Touhey. Agianst Newton Friday night, the seniors standouts proved their worth.

With Benz taking charge one half and Touhey the other, Dover had little trouble scalping the Braves, 55-45, in this Iron Area Conference game which put the Tigers into undisputed possession of second place over Newton.

The dynamic duo gets some ink with this article written at the end of our senior season. Danny and I were formidable opponents for the opposing teams to contend with.

The four lifelong friends at a wedding-anniversary celebration in the early 1990s. Pictured (left to right) are David, Danny, me, and Mike.

The terrific trio in the mid-1990s.

This picture was taken around 2003 at a restaurant in Lake Hopatcong. Standing on the outdoor deck *(left to right)* are David, me, Danny, and Mike.

```
MINOR LEAGUE
Mt. Arlington FD. ..............12        2
Rickels .......................11        3
Glamour Cleaners ............8        5
LL. VFW. ....................7        6
Sam's Sonoco ...............7        7
Succs. Chem. ...............5        9
Center Pharmacy ..........2       11
Nunzio's Barber ...........1       12
```

The final standings for the 1961 Roxbury Little
League. We were the champs!

Forty-six years after winning the Roxbury Little League championship, I
find the abandoned ball field behind St. Theresa's Church in Kenvil, New
Jersey. Serena takes a picture of me standing by the fence where my father
stood when he watched me play in 1961.

The 1963 Mt. Fern Dairy baseball team at King's field in Dover. That's me in the front row with the big smile on my face holding the baseball.

In 1964 I was a member of the Dover Little League All-Star Team. I am in the second row, second from right.

As a player at CCM in 1971, I posed for this publicity photo. The picture accompanied an article written about me towards the end of my freshman season. The headline was a nice compliment.

'HANGING AROUND' PAYS OFF'

Touhey Tough Young Titan

the players...

kevin touhey

The surprise of the season...the 6-0 freshman was figured as sixth or seventh man in preseason drills but started 23 of 25 games...405 points for season and 34-point performance against Keystone CCM records...led team in scoring, average (16.2) and field goal percentage (52.2)...gets a lot of points by being "where the ball is" and has a good outside jump shot...hard worker, always looking to improve his game...plans to spend summer sharpening ball-handling and defensive skills...Dover High graduate...

COUNTY COLLEGE of Morris basketball coach Jack Martin still raving about defensive job Kevin Touhey (Dover High grad) did on Essex County College's scoring machine Aron Stewart . . . Stewart, averaging close to 35 ppg, was held to 14 by Touhey last week in Morris' 70-66 upset victory over Essex . . . Touhey scored 19 . . . Morris still trails Marshall Brown's team by one-half game in the race for the Northern Division title of the Garden State Athletic Conference . . .

These two pieces feature a small blurb about the job I did to cover Aron Stewart and a summary of my basketball accomplishments my freshman year in college.

A Touhey family Thanksgiving dinner in the mid-1960s. On the left, partially hidden, is Dad. Around the table *(left to right)* are me, Brian, Dennis, Eileen, Tim, Mom, Mike, Pat, Mimi, and Maureen. My guess is that Kathy took the picture.

The boys in full uniform pose in the backyard of our house in Dover: *(left to right)* Mike, Pat, and Tim across the front, Dennis, me, Dad, and Brian in back. This picture was probably taken in 1968.

A familiar place for me to be—on my father's right-hand side. This picture was taken on Christmas Day, maybe 1971, with Dad holding his gifts.

Another backyard pose around 1971–72. Pat, Tim, and Mike are in the front row. Behind them in the back row are Dad, me with my arm around him, Eileen, and Brian.

Me and Dad watching a football game at Aunt Agnes's house, 1968.

This picture was taken on Christmas Day in 1963. A sparse Christmas tree in the background tells of a struggling family.

The Touhey children at a family party in the late 1980s. In the front row *(left to right)* are Pat, Tim, and Mike. Standing in the back row are Kathy, Maureen, Eileen, me, Brian, and Dennis.

PART
4

APPRECIATION

Appreciation is that feeling that you are appreciated for who you are, not for what you can do or have accomplished. I would rate my experience of being appreciated somewhere in the middle on the scale of 1 to 10—perhaps a 4. Most of the appreciation came from earning it by some performance. Consequently, it was very conditional.

However, there were times when I felt I was truly appreciated for who I was as a person regardless of whether or not I was earning it. I'll share a few stories here that illustrate such pure appreciation.

I'll also share other stories in which if I was not performing according to what someone else thought was right, I was shown no appreciation at all.

You'll see how my experiences average out to that middle-of-the-road score.

11

The Miracle of Little League: Feeling Fully Appreciated

"THE DEEPEST PRINCIPLE IN HUMAN NATURE
IS THE CRAVING TO BE APPRECIATED."
— *William James*

My official playing career began in the Roxbury Little League in 1961. I played for the Mount Arlington Fire Department team. Other than my father, this coach was my first official coach, and he was a great guy. He told me I was really good, the best player on the team next to Tommy Thomas. I was so proud when he said I would play shortstop and be number three in the batting order. After practice one day, he walked me over to my dad and said to him, "Jim, you have a very talented son. He could play any position on the field." My dad was proud. He said, "Thanks, I know he loves to play."

While my father watched me play his favorite game, I was reliving some of his pain over Regina's death. Starring in the Roxbury Little League gave him a healthy diversion from the haunting thoughts of her passing. As I am writing, I remember that I felt fearful of performing with a uniform on, just as I had when I was five in the Bloomfield Little League.

I am glad Mr. Granada was the coach. He lived right around the corner and drove me to the games. He made sure I had a soda after the games. He always told me I was a good player. With all the Touhey family had been through the winter of 1960–61, being good in Little League baseball felt awfully good. The team was tied for first place with only a few games left in the season. It really felt great to be part of this team and I felt appreciated by Mr. Granada and my teammates.

> *Gratitude and appreciation are key elements to tapping into your true power. These two simple feeling states are a pathway to building a joyful, happy, abundant, optimistic life, right here and right now.*

Once again the inconsistency of my young life reared its ugly head, just when I felt so comfortable in being part of the team. My mom and dad announced that we were moving from Mount Arlington. We were looking for a home back in Essex County, but for a short time we were staying with the Ryersons in Dover. I had to attend East Dover School for the last three weeks of school. I was heartbroken.

When I told Mr. Granada I was moving and would not be there for the championship run, he hatched a plan. He told my father that no one needed to know we were moving. Mr. Granada said he would drive to Dover and pick me up for the remaining games. I was told not to say a word of this to anyone. I felt pretty darn important and terrifically appreciated for my playing skills. It was such a kick that Coach would drive to Dover to pick me up for the games. The feeling of belonging and appreciation placed me on top of the world. His gesture also provided some consistency in yet another unstable period of time.

This was the second time in my short life that I was told not to say anything that might get us in trouble while wearing a baseball uniform. The first time was when I was five years old in Bloomfield, playing in the eight year old league. Now it was five years later, playing in the Roxbury Little League under shady circumstances.

My confidence level soared. I remember sitting on the curb in front of the Ryersons' house on Penn Avenue in Dover waiting for Mr. Granada to pick me up. I eagerly anticipated seeing him and my teammates, especially Tommy Thomas. I grinned from ear to ear while I waited to see Coach's car coming over the crest of the steep hill. All the feeling of stability I had was wrapped up in his arrival. Wearing the red uniform of the Mount Arlington Fire Department was one of the only bright lights in my life.

Since the Ryersons and the Touheys each had eight children, there were about twenty people living in the house. It was so crowded, people all over the place. Being on the playing field was my salvation. I thank God that Mr. Granada went out of his way to come and get me so I could continue to play.

We won the last couple of games. It may be a small thing, but I remember after one of the games Coach said we had to stop at the grocery store to get a few things before he took me back to Dover. I was so proud walking around the store with him in my red uniform. A couple of people asked if we had won the game. I proudly said yes. My heart was filled with pride. I felt great. I felt important and my family's turbulent lifestyle seemed far away. In my uniform I was insulated from the fears I felt at home. One store patron asked, "Hey, win, lose, or draw?" Mr. Granada asked me, "Aren't you going to answer?" I replied, "I don't know what draw means." They both laughed and I laughed too. It is funny how such small details are stored away in memory. I even remember the store. Although it's no longer a supermarket, whenever I drive by the location, all of those good emotional memories come flooding back.

I was immensely aware, even back then, that I should pay attention and feel good about these seemingly minor human exchanges. I held onto the good feelings that these incidents gave a little boy with monumental challenges. I was learning that human interaction could bring joy as well as pain. Paying attention to these moments provided a good foundation for remaining hopeful in life. I sometimes forgot that truth, as the conditions and circumstances of my life dimmed the view a little, but I never totally forgot. And I remember them all now.

In the first lesson in this book you read about self-awareness. It is that level of awareness that reconnected me to the spirit in these human interactions. What circumstances of ego-based living have buried your own self-awareness? What pearls of joy could you uncover that might provide a measure of happiness that you currently can't access? When you're detached from your own awareness of potential happiness, it affects you on a spiritual level.

My daughter Serena and I recently went back to the site of the Roxbury Little League field that sat behind the old St. Theresa's Church. To find the spot where the field had been, we fought through the overgrown brush. It hadn't been used for twenty years. It was exhilarating to find that place! The flood of emotion was overwhelming for me. Serena yelled, "Dad, what an excursion, this is the best play date ever." I am sure she picked up the feeling of pure joy I experienced having located the field.

The fence that surrounded the playing field was intact. There was an opening in the fence where someone had broken the chain link. Serena and I went onto the old playing field through that opening. I said to her, "Honey, we are going to find some remaining structure— a dugout or the old concession stand." I was determined to find some solid piece of the past that had stood the test of time. After about five minutes we came upon the old first-base dugout buried under trees and brush. "We found it, Dad, let's take some pictures," Serena bellowed. Then she asked, "What's a dugout?" I enjoyed explaining the function of a dugout to my little girl.

Serena and I were able to trace the field locations once we'd found the dugout. "Here is home plate, honey," I said. "Hey, this is where the shortstop position is located, Serena. That was the position Daddy played on this field." I asked her if she remembered playing shortstop during her T-ball season. "I remember, Dad," she responded. "This is so cool, Dad."

> *A childlike exuberance gives the heart a feeling of thanks and joy. That particular type of awe is a bio-spiritual phenomenon.*

While standing where I stood playing shortstop forty-five years earlier, I glanced to my right, where my father used to watch me play. Tears streamed down my face as I realized that the very spot where my dad stood was where the chain link was broken. The only access point for Serena and me to step back into the past and into the heart and spirit of my father's presence was right there behind third base. A sense of peace came over me when I heard my daughter's little voice right beside me. "Dad, do you want to take a picture of where Grandpa Touhey used to stand?" I said, "Yes, Serena, let's go over and take a picture." "This is great, Dad," Serena said. I agreed, "The best, honey, just the best." Mr. Granada helped rekindle hope in me that tomorrow could always be a better day. It is easy to see why sports held a place of such importance to me. By playing the rest of the season, I was able to see that if I was hopeful, something good would happen. This time when we moved, I had a glimmer of optimism because of Mr. Granada.

One Saturday we were playing the Rickel's Hardware team for the championship of the Roxbury Little League. They had yellow uniforms. I can remember my father in his familiar location leaning up against the fence down the third base line. Coach walked over with me and again told my dad I was good enough to play anywhere on the field. I know my dad was proud. That moment is such a strong emotional memory for me because I was being appreciated for my talent. I was also part of the team and it felt good to belong.

Although my father wasn't putting inordinate pressure on me, I was nervous before the game. We were up first and I can see myself waiting for my turn at bat in the first inning. Their pitcher was really good and he threw hard. I batted third in the order, so I knew I was going to get up to bat in the first inning. Tommy batted fourth. We watched our first two teammates get blown away as we waited our turn.

As I walked up to the plate, I glanced down at my father as he leaned against the fence on the third-base line. He was cheering me on to get a hit. I really felt his encouragement and that helped me to relax a little bit. He wasn't yelling, just cheering. Still, I felt the pressure. I was desperate to get a hit.

I loved my father and wanted to please him. To have him encourage me, rather than put pressure on me, was such a contrast to most experiences I had while playing ball. The look on his face gave me the confidence that I could hit against this pitcher. Juxtaposed against the nearly constant angst and strife in our family over so many things, this isolated moment suspended the pain, even if just for a moment. That became the pattern in the years to come. Athletic success was used to cover major problems and suppress a world of pain. This fine moment that seemed just right provided a small oasis of peace in the very stormy world of the Touhey family.

In this particular moment, as I glanced down the third baseline, I saw my dad cheering me on. This man had taught me and so many young boys to play sports. Recently my cousin Joe was talking to me at a family party. He told me that in a conversation with a friend he had said what great baseball teachers he had growing up. He said to his friend that he had Hoddy McHon, Joe Gravy, and his Uncle Jimmy (my dad) teach him the right way to play ball. Even now at age fifty-five, my heart filled with love and admiration for my father as my cousin acknowledged that. It made me proud and reminded me of my father's love of sports. It reminded me that in the purity of his soul, my dad loved Joe because he was family and that was important to him. It showed me that my cousin Joe really knew deep down inside that Uncle Jimmy, with all the demons he fought, cared enough to take the time to teach Joe how to play baseball.

> *When you learn to generate a state of heartfelt thanks in all conditions, situations, circumstances, and negative states of emotion, it becomes an exercise in taking responsibility for your responses to all the circumstances in your life. Now that's powerful!*

I stepped into the batter's box reinforced by my father's encouragement. The pitcher did not seem so imposing now. After two balls, he delivered a pitch that was very fast, but I got the bat around enough to drive the ball toward the gap in right center field. As I rounded second base and headed toward third, the coach told me to hold up. I saw my dad standing behind the fence cheering me on. Tommy came up next and got a hit to drive me in. As I crossed home plate, I felt that rush come over me that happens with such a proud moment of accomplishment. I would have this rush many times in my athletic career. It's a great feeling—there is nothing wrong with feeling good due to the pride of accomplishment. But the self-confidence that I felt got married to that rush of accomplishment that day and I continued to confuse conditional self-confidence with true self-esteem for many years to come. I began to live for that rush.

On a lighter note, we went on to win the game and the championship! The post-game celebration included huge hugs from the coach and my dad. But the real treat was that the team was allowed to order anything we wanted from the concession stand, courtesy of Mrs. Thomas. It was a grand celebration!

We moved from the Ryersons' house later that summer. The team was awarded trophies for winning the championship. It took months for me to get my trophy. We were living in Glen Ridge when it finally showed up. In my mind's eye I can see myself showing it off to my cousins Joe and Rob. The trophy went on the mantel in the living room for all to see, a symbol of the championship we had won.

The trophy was the first of many earned by the Touhey boys. Those trophies became one of the sole sources of pride and ego identification for our entire family. They proved to the world that the Touhey family was worthy. The young men earning the trophies were now responsible for making sure they kept coming. Eventually these badges of honor for the Touheys would adorn an entire table. Upon entering our home in Dover, most people noticed the trophy table decorating the foyer first of all.

The number and growing complexity of the financial, emotional, and spiritual problems in the household could not be overcome by athletic prowess. For the boys especially, competing became the temporary healing tonic that tempered the intensity of the family's pain. My father cultivated that culture within the family.

His need to have something outside of himself as a source for his self-esteem was born in his own upbringing. The lack of appreciation and the lack of belonging in a safe community sent my dad searching for something to hold onto. The athletic accomplishments of his children became that something, his sole source of esteem.

LESSON 8

INTENTIONAL APPRECIATION

Gratitude and appreciation are the power tools to build a joyful, happy, abundant, optimistic life. This can be done right here and now. Learning to generate these feelings in real time, no matter how the situation appears, is a key concept in healing and releasing old wounds and perceived problems. When you develop the practical and spiritual tools of being grateful and appreciative for all that comes your way, you are on your way to a blissful, energy-packed life.

This state of appreciation provides the basis for the merging of mind, body, and spirit. This integration provides a powerful platform to launch an optimistic being. The energy that comes from a heart filled with thanks and awe is a bio-spiritual phenomenon.

In the first exercise in this book you were guided through a process of identifying negative feeling states in your life right now. The time has come to put the low-energy feeling states, such as fear, anxiety, hate, judgment, frustration, and worry, to rest. They may have served you well, but it is time to shed some light on the dark shadow sides of your existence. We all have them.

From this moment on, you will use appreciation and gratitude to help you become a being living in a state of grace. In this heart-centered state of appreciation, you will replace blame with self-responsibility. In fact, if you bring a state of heartfelt thanks to all negative states of emotion, situations, circumstances, and conditions, all blame melts away. Self-pity and feelings of victim-hood also dissolve. The rest of the exercises in the book are intended to transform any negative feeling states to positive at the moment they occur.

The simple bio-spiritual truth is that you cannot experience appreciation at the same time you are experiencing worry, shame, anger, or any other negative feeling. It's not physically possible. And you can't just sweep the negatives under the rug. That rug becomes a cellular storage bank, and those feelings will come back to haunt you. They must be transformed instead.

From the following exercise you will learn the ability to change your emotions in real time. Thinking, and generating a positive feeling in your heart about your thoughts, will give you that ability. It is simple. It is a freewill decision, a choice of whether or not to stay stuck. Positive emotions are measurably 100 percent more powerful than negative. It takes a lot of energy to continually process negative emotions.

To truly transform your life into one of unbridled optimism, it is important to awaken to how you are feeling. This awareness state, this monitoring of your feelings, is a crucial element of this process.

All new learning and change is created in the present. It is imperative to understand that point. If you stay aware of it, you will transform your entire life. Being aware of how your present state of being affects your energy and vibrancy, you'll view any past grievances with a different, clearer, more focused perspective. Einstein noted the folly of trying to solve problems with the same mind that created the problem. If you are trying to generate a good feeling about something negative in your past or present experience, it will be difficult, if not impossible, to do it from a state of negativity toward the situation. It takes positive states of acceptance, enjoyment, and enthusiasm to resolve any issues from the past. When I speak of the past, I am talking about any period of time that is not RIGHT NOW!

Even if your life is functioning fairly well but lacks a little of the zest and zeal you desire, gratitude and appreciation, generated on purpose and with intention, will ignite your soul like nothing else.

We live in a very stressful and fast-paced society. It's easy to accumulate negative emotions from the little day-to-day interruptions of peace in our lives. Gratitude and appreciation will help us look at those interruptions as a gift.

It was learning to use gratitude and appreciation within a practical ritual that helped me deal with all the situations of the past in this book. I was able to snatch the pearl out of each and every incident by ritualizing the feeling state of appreciation.

LESSON 9

THE VALUE OF APPRECIATION AND GRATITUDE:

THINKING, ACTIVATING, FEELING

- Appreciation combines thankfulness, admiration, and gratitude.
- Scientists have discovered that appreciation is one of the easiest and most powerful positive feelings to activate.
- When an individual taps into the positive feelings of appreciation, he allows himself the chance to see the big picture. This is true even in very stressful moments.
- Each person has the ability to reach the highest level of her potential when she is connected to more positive, heartfelt states like appreciation and gratitude.
- Activating appreciation and gratitude allows you to be confident, alert, and totally focused, maintaining high levels of energy.
- In a coherent state of being, you are better able to concentrate on the process and journey of life without regard or attachment to the outcome of situations.

Appreciation is a super power tool for your own growth. Appreciating *what is,* rather than focusing on and complaining about *what isn't,* helps you make peace in the moment. Appreciation is also one of the easiest heart frequencies to shift into. You'll feel the difference fast.

Exercise 8

ACTIVATING APPRECIATION

1. Write a list of people who engender a feeling of appreciation in you.

_____

_____

_____

_____

_____

2. Pick one person from the list. Complete the following statement. What I appreciate most about you is:

_____

_____

_____

_____

_____

3. List all the qualities of that person that you appreciate.

_____

_____

_____

_____

_____

STEPS TO BREATHING IN OPTIMISM

1. Take three deep breaths through your mouth. Breathe deep into your abdomen. Feel your stomach rise and deflate with each breathe.

2. Take three deep breaths through your mouth and fill your chest. Feel your chest rise and deflate with each breath.

3. Picture your heart in your mind's eye. Focus on the center of your chest. As you continue to breathe in a relaxed fashion, focus on your heart.

4. As you think about the things you appreciate about that one person, continue to focus on your heart and feel the warm sensation that fills your being. Keep that feeling present as you continue to breathe.

5. If your mind wanders, gently bring your focus back to your heart. Do not judge yourself if you cannot quiet your mind. Gently favor the area around your heart and continue to appreciate and breathe.

WHAT'S YOUR STORY?

Please journal about any new insights you've come to in this lesson. In what ways are you overlooking chances to be grateful? What conditions and circumstances do you think you could experience differently if you viewed them through a lens of appreciation?

_____

_____

_____

_____

_____

12

The Other Side of the Coin: Feeling No Appreciation

"BASEBALL WAS MADE FOR KIDS, AND
GROWN-UPS ONLY SCREW IT UP."
— *Bob Lemon, former major-league baseball pitcher*

I played Little League baseball in Dover, New Jersey, for the Mt. Fern Dairy team. This was the same dairy where my dad was a truck driver when we lived in Mount Arlington. I was the youngest pitcher on the team. My coach, Mr. Morris, was a great guy.

In the preseason Mr. Morris asked my dad to work with the pitchers. The first day I went to practice at Hedden Park, the two of them struck up a conversation. Dad told him his background, and Mr. Morris immediately said he would love for Dad to help.

Mr. Morris had built a pitcher's mound in his backyard. Rich Apples, Ronny Shapiro, and I were the pitchers. Dick Dentson practiced with us because he was the team's main catcher.

I was really proud of my dad. He loved to teach and he was so patient with all of us. He knew how to teach baseball. He changed the way Rich wound up to pitch, which really helped him become a dominant pitcher in the league. I loved going there to work on pitching with my dad. He never raised his voice during these teaching sessions. I understood what my cousin Joe meant when he said my dad was a great teacher of baseball.

Of course that mood wasn't consistent and my dad defaulted to angry behavior once the season began. It was in Dover Little League where my father started a pattern of nothing-is-ever-good-enough. A mistake was unacceptable. Eventually, even perfection was unacceptable.

I still loved to train and practice because I could relax. But for the rest of my playing career, I would never relax totally while playing in a game.

> *When driving a car, you have a destination that requires a certain route. Goals are the road maps that give your life direction.*

It was my first year playing with the big boys in the major division of the league. Early in the year, I was asked to pitch against a very good team, National Union Bank. The team wore red uniforms. I did not know him then, but my dear friend Dave Loeb was on the team. The game was played at Crescent Field, right by my house. It was a bright, sunny Saturday afternoon, a great day for a game. My dad stood at the top of the hill watching as I walked to the mound in the top of the first. Dick yelled for me to relax and just throw strikes. I blew the first batter away with three pitches, the second batter on three pitches, and the third on three pitches. I threw a total of nine pitches and I could hear the buzz from the stands. Who was this young kid? What a pitcher!

The feeling was amazing. I really liked the rush I got from people's talk about me and my skills. Mr. Morris came up to me in between innings and told me I had done my job and we really needed to win this game to stay in contention for first place. He told me he was going to put Rich and Ronnie in over the last five innings. I was moved to shortstop. I did not complain. I was happy to have done my job.

The first batter to face Rich got a hit. I could see my father on the top of the hill pacing back and forth. He was not happy. The second batter struck out. The next batter hit a ball right up the middle. I got a jump on it and caught the ball in the gap, tagged second base to get that runner, and threw to first for a double play. I sprinted to the bench while the crowd once again buzzed with delight at my exploits. My self-confidence was at an all-time high. But I looked up at my dad and all I saw was an angry man.

I was being slapped on the back by everyone on the team. I had shown the team that I was not going to pout because I'd been taken out as a pitcher earlier in the game. My father exhibited nothing but disgust at the coach. The appreciation for my talent and the surreal feeling of belonging to this team of older guys was now tempered by the unreal expectations of a father looking for his own happiness through the exploits of his Little Leaguer. He had rained on the parade.

When we got home I experienced the first of a long line of rants about how I was being slighted by the coaches. I knew on a very deep level that my dad was wrong. No one was out to get me and no one was trying to slight me. This wasn't the rejection of his own father wrapped up in the persona of Mr. Morris. This was not his own father leaving him. This was Mr. Morris doing his best to win a game and keep the team in contention for first place. The sins of my father's father were slipping into my playing career in Little League.

Coach gave me the opportunity to pitch in a really big game against the best team in the league, H.O. Baker. I was slated to pitch against the best pitcher in the entire league, Eddie DiMarco. The stands were filled, my dad was in the front row, it was a beautiful day, and I was very nervous. I had a bad cold and a fever. But there was no way I was going to miss this game.

In the very first inning I got two quick outs and then big Frank Bass stepped up to the plate. Rich Apples was playing third base for us. My dad had tried to convince me that I should watch out for him and Ronnie Shapiro because they were older players who wanted to be pitching in this big game. Well, Frank got a hit and now I was going to have to face the best player in the league, Eddie DiMarco. On the first pitch he popped up in foul territory behind third base and was running out what was surely going to be the last out of the inning.

NO WAY!! Rich dropped the easy fly ball and Eddie was kept alive. I did the worst thing I could have done—I glanced over at my father. He was shaking his head, telling himself that Rich had a conspiracy going to make sure I didn't get my share of the fame. I heard my father yelling to get this guy out. The next pitch was called a ball, though I still think it hit the inside corner of the plate. The next pitch Eddie hit so far over the left-field fence that I am sure forty-five years later it is still traveling. That quickly, it was a home run, 2-0, H.O. Baker.

I turned away from where my father was sitting and fought back the tears. I thought to myself, that SOB, Rich Apples, he should have caught that ball. Mr. Morris stepped out of the dugout and came to the mound to try and settle me down. The first thing I said to him was that I was sick and maybe someone else should come in to pitch. Then I started to cry.

As I turned around I saw my father running to the mound. When he got to the mound, he called me a baby and a quitter. Coach chased him from the mound, encouraged me to finish the inning, and headed back to the dugout. I struck out the last batter, and in the next inning I played shortstop and Rich pitched.

I had a great game. I overcame the problems I had faced in the first inning and had three base hits and two great plays in the field. But in my father's belief system I had not overcome anything. What I had done, in his mind, was QUIT. I know I felt good about coming back and playing the rest of the game well. But I began to wonder, *Am I a quitter?* I kept that feeling for a very long time, even though it was not the truth. Actually, it was quite the opposite; I didn't throw in the towel. After a tough start I came back strong.

> *Many people pull up short of achieving their goals because they're afraid of failing. They give up too soon. It is important to use fear to propel rather than paralyze. Overcoming fear by staying committed, persistent, and consistent can provide the emotional intensity needed to support your goal attainment.*

I was delivering papers the next Monday and stopped to collect from one of my customers. An older kid opened the door when I knocked. He started to laugh and said, "Hey, aren't you the kid who was crying on the mound on Saturday?" A flood of shame washed over me as I explained to him that I was sick. I asked him if he'd seen the rest of the game when I played well. His response was that we lost the game and that was all that mattered. As I walked away, I internalized the belief that it was my fault.

I let that negative experience affect my own belief system and self-confidence for a long time. I began to raise the bar for what it would take to make me feel even conditional self-confidence. I was beginning to set myself up not to feel goal satisfaction. But goal satisfaction is an essential element of self-confidence. You can't build self-esteem without it.

To my father, mistakes and failure were one and the same. I may have made a pitching mistake and given Eddie a good pitch to hit over the fence. But I was no failure. I did my best and gave it my all. It was not a lazy pitch. In addition to that, I overcame the adversity of that mistake and played five great innings of baseball. Had my father been able to say, "You challenged yourself and used that to have a great game," that might've helped me believe something more positive about myself.

When the All-Star team was picked that year, I was not chosen. But I wasn't upset. The only other player in the league my age who was chosen was Bobby McElwaine, who played for Dover Trust. Bobby was better than me. I thought he deserved to be chosen. Well, my dad went nuts when he found out that Rich and Ronnie made the team. They were both two grades ahead of me. They were more physically developed and they were both better than me. I was picked as an alternate. I was proud of that.

But my father ranted about how I got cheated. He told me that Mr. Morris could have gotten me on the All-Star team but he just liked the other boys better. I knew this wasn't true. Mr. Morris loved me. I told my dad that what had happened was fair. I told him that I was glad a kid my age was picked as an alternate to the team. I told him I was sure to be one of the top two or three players in the whole league the next year.

His anger with the situation now turned from the adults, who he was sure all got together in a smoke-filled room to conspire to keep me off the All-Star team, and was directed at me. My father yelled at me for accepting the fact that anyone was any better than me. He called me a coward for not standing up to Mr. Morris and telling him how I felt. In my mind, though, the right choice had been made. It was my father who was upset.

When you're young you begin to doubt what you believe to be true when an adult tells you that you're wrong. This was one of the many instances in my life where I was told not to trust what I knew intuitively to be true. Since I am a natural intuitive, I was being set up to mistrust my own instincts. I was told that reality lay outside of what I knew was true. My self-esteem took a big blow in these instances. I wondered if I could trust myself to know what was real. What was I not seeing? Were all these men and boys and their families out to get the Touhey family and me?

Today I teach my own children to respect what they feel and think. I am not right about their world just because I am older or because I'm their father. But my father's low self-esteem made him tell me I should not trust anyone. So I sometimes doubted what my own instincts and intuition were telling me. The result was a lifelong struggle to discern what was true about people, places, and things and what wasn't. The facts according to my father were that people in charge did not really like me because I was a Touhey; they were jealous; I was good enough to be on the All-Star team, but they were keeping me off. He tried very hard to make me believe that falsehood.

I was sitting on the steps in the foyer while he went on and on about this. I can see my brothers sitting in the living room listening. The truth was that I was respected as one of the best young players in the league. Mr. Morris told me after our last game that I would tear the league up next year. I had that in my mind as I picked up the phone to tell him how upset I was that he didn't get me placed on the All-Star team. The script my father told me to recite included that Mr. Morris liked Rich and Ronnie better and that is why he got them on the team.

Mr. Morris sounded bewildered and then angry. He told me that he had recommended me as an alternate. He said Rick and Ronnie had just played their last year in the league and they deserved to be the first ones chosen. He told me that they were better.

My father stood next to the radiator in the foyer. That's where the phone was in those days. I was in fifth or sixth grade and talking on the phone with a coach I loved. I was standing next to my first coach—the father I loved. Mr. Morris said I should not be so selfish. He said that if I was head and shoulders better than those two guys, the league would have chosen me. I knew he was right.

When I hung up, I told my father what he said. My father called him a liar. I remember Brian standing in the doorway between the foyer and the living room while my father yelled about not trusting anyone. My insides were all bunched up and mentally I said to Brian, *Don't listen.* The episode ended with my father saying I better get better if I was going to make the All-Star team next year.

I'd had a great season, but the feeling of confidence I earned from that season was washed away in the foyer of 167 Penn Avenue. That foyer, which housed one lone trophy at the time, would soon house dozens more earned by all the Touhey boys. The shame I felt that night in the foyer would be masked by the many symbols of accomplishment for all to see. Unfortunately, the low self-esteem I felt could not be washed away by all the plastic and metal statues in the world.

Creative goal-setting can help erase the past.

13

The Miracle of Becoming President: Contrasting Appreciation and Lack

"APPRECIATION IS A WONDERFUL THING.
IT MAKES WHAT IS EXCELLENT IN OTHERS
BELONG TO US AS WELL."

— *Voltaire*

I went to Sacred Heart in Dover for grades five (second round) through eight. I struggled academically in every school I attended after we moved from Newark Avenue. However, I did become one of the most popular boys in the school at Sacred Heart in Dover.

In eighth grade, I was elected class president. Sister Eileen instituted an electoral system whereby each student had a popular vote and an electoral vote, just like the real presidential elections. She was beside herself with grief when her prize student, Kenny Carford, lost the election. There were about fifty students in the eighth grade and I was third to last in class rank in academic standing. Since Sister had us sit in rows according to our rank, it was easy for the whole class to see that the president-elect was seated in the last row, third from the end, with his girl buddies. I am sure Sister nearly burnt up a set of rosary beads asking God why He let me get elected president. My slogan was "Vote for Red (my hair) and You Won't Be Blue." However, for Sister Eileen, "you won't be blue" but downright depressed was more like it.

But I'd won the election handily, so to question the results or ask for a recount would be too obvious a ploy to unseat me.

I was feeling pretty good about myself. I had gone from being the new kid three years earlier to winning the presidency in a landslide. I knew that at the very least I was likable, even if my grades were among the worst in the class. I picked Danny Franks to be my vice president. He wasn't as popular as I, but he sat in the first row with all the smart students so I thought he balanced the ticket.

We needed that balance since I had chosen my academic equal, Sharon Bosworth, as my secretary. Sharon's seat in the classroom was next to the last. I'm sure Sister Eileen was trying to bring to light every sin Sharon ever committed in case she hadn't asked for forgiveness yet. Sister was experiencing hell right here on earth with Sharon on my governing team. Sharon wore a leather jacket to school every day and every day Sister yelled at her that it wasn't appropriate. Sharon was physically mature beyond her years and I'm sure it was a sin to look at her! But she was my secretary now and there was nothing the good Sister could do about it.

Sister had tried her best to influence the vote. The little warrior in me not only campaigned to win the election, but wanted to win the war in my soul, to overcome the feelings of rejection that came from knowing the adult in charge wanted me to lose. So when I won, I felt happy and unworthy at the same time. That paradoxical feeling state became very familiar to me. Situations like these, where I did not know which feeling was real, became a breeding ground for a lifelong struggle with anxiety.

I carried all but a few "states" and, as Sister posted the popular vote on the blackboard, I thought her habit was going to pop right off her head! She had a hard time concealing her anger at the class for the way they'd voted and her disdain for the new eighth-grade class president, Kevin M. Touhey. I was smiling on the outside, but I couldn't help but think that maybe she was right and the smart kid should have won. That duality robbed me of any real joy. Whenever I won awards, I always had a much muted feeling of happiness that quickly dissipated in the pressure of whatever I had to accomplish next. I never felt much goal satisfaction. I have seen many people in my coaching practice who suffer from that same affliction.

As my presidential term began, Sister put time aside each week for a full class meeting to discuss the pressing issues that arise in eighth grade! One of the tenets of my campaign platform was that we deal with the issues of the class, but suspend formalities and make it fun. Sister insisted we use parliamentary procedure at all times. I protested, pointing out that I had won the election and I should be able to bring that issue to a vote with the entire class participating. Then Sister gave me a very valuable lesson on the limitations of democracy: she made a unilateral decision that I would under no circumstances bring this matter up for a vote. My good old VP, Danny Franks, sat in silence as Sister and I had this discussion. I understood that he was trying to balance his loyalty to me and his fear of repercussion from her. But she'd won and that was final.

I froze every time I ran the meetings. As I feared forgetting some procedure, my mind just stopped. Danny knew the procedures, so initially I deferred to him when I got stuck. I began losing the confidence I'd had during the campaign. The creative ideas I had about new kinds of class projects and new ways to conduct spelling bees got buried under an avalanche of policies and procedures.

Rather than encouraging my creative strength, Sister highlighted my procedural weakness. Danny and I could have conducted meetings with me throwing out idea after idea and him making sure the class discussed and voted on them properly. Instead, I felt stupid in front of the same classmates I'd won over with my speeches during the campaign. At the start of each meeting, I truly felt like the kid who had to sit in the last row of the classroom because of his bad grades. The conditional confidence I had from winning the election was being replaced by shame.

But somewhere in my subconscious was a guiding spirit telling me to keep fighting. The spirit of hope planted a long time ago was alive whether I was aware of it or not. I was able to fight through the feelings of shame to take the actions I needed, because I knew on a gut level that something better was right around the corner if I persisted. That is the definition of hope, after all.

Still, I began to hate running the meetings and I lost all confidence. I went to Sister and told her that I would run most of the meeting and would consult Danny when some more formal procedure was in order. She told me I had violated the trust the class had in me. She was really having some fun at my expense now. Then she said that I was an academic failure and I constantly flirted with the class hussies. Next, out came the big guns as she explained that my disregard for the standards and rules of the office were grounds for impeachment. I'm willing to bet I was the only eighth-grade president in the history of grammar-school politics to be tried for an impeachable offense.

She'd banned listening to the Barry McGuire song "Eve of Destruction." I was familiar with some of the words. I liked the beat of the song, so I listened to it. I can see myself on the phone in the kitchen with Danny asking him to give me all the words. He was a musician, so he knew the words to a lot of songs. I wrote the words as he spoke them and the song made sense to me. The songwriter's theory was that we needed to change as human beings and treat each other better or we were going to destroy the world. I asked Sister the next day why we Catholics weren't allowed to listen to a song with a seemingly Christian message. The words were not unlike the words that Jesus himself had spoken.

She hit the roof. Now insubordination was added to the list of offenses racked up by this wayward president who did not know parliamentary procedure. Sister told me it was time to write my resignation speech. I refused and told her she was going to have to impeach me to get me out of office. So she began the process and included the whole class. I had to give a speech defending myself.

I do not know what Sister Eileen's life was like growing up. She was very angry with those of us who didn't fit her definition of a good child. I had not done anything malicious or disrespectful to make her dislike me so intensely. She wanted me out of office and that was that.

There were a few things she did not know about me. By the time I was in eighth grade, I had been through some very difficult times in my life. I already knew what it was to feel shame and I definitely felt shame during this whole episode. She wasn't the first adult in my life to measure my worth by some condition or circumstance. I had been through some pretty intense training in the area of adverse situations. She did not know that I could feel shame, be judged and labeled, and still find the fortitude to work my way around and through the challenges I faced. She was at a distinct disadvantage. I was afraid, but fear wouldn't stop me from fighting.

Sister decided to use the system of electoral votes just as in the general election. I knew I was going to lose votes because Sister had presented a pretty strong case to the class against me. She told the class they had let the first vote become a popularity contest. "And this mess is what you got," she said. I realized I could lose the popular vote and still win the electoral vote. I would need some of the key states to vote my way if I was going to continue as President Touhey.

I'd learned to survive much more dire conditions than this in my life. No one in the class knew that on the cold winter night before the vote, my sisters, brothers, and I were huddled in front of the stove in the kitchen to stay warm in a house that had no oil for the furnace. We were eating the famous "buns" that were a staple for the Touhey family when times were tough. Buns consisted of flour and water baked to perfection in the oven. They tasted terrible but filled the stomach. I slept that night with my winter coat on and I could see my breath. I felt cold, I felt shame, I hoped our family would get some money and I was sad for me and my family. Nevertheless, I was determined to overcome all that, defend my honor, and keep the office I had won.

> *Knowing your strengths and identifying your limitations gives insight into who you are. That, in turn, can affect your attitude. Successful people build on their strengths and are not overly concerned about their limitations. Develop a positive attitude that trains your mind to look at lim itations as a ground discovery—a discovery that can be the basis for powerful responses that develop strength, power, and greatness.*

In spite of feeling that I had failed to uphold the office the way Sister wanted it, I proceeded with a plan to save my presidency. Sister had told the class that if I was impeached, her hero, Kenny, that beacon for all that was good, would assume office. Since Danny always had money, I told him that he was going to fund a little gathering for the bigger states with a lot of electoral votes. We would take them around the corner from Sacred Heart School the day before the impeachment vote and treat them to pizza while I pleaded my case for keeping my office.

We told our little gathering we really wanted to stay in office and what Sister was doing was unfair. Without the restrictions of parliamentary procedure, I was able to eloquently present our case. I had run on a platform of less formal class meetings that were fun. I reminded them that they had voted me in—in a landslide—on that plank of my platform. I asked them to remember that the next day when they voted. I also asked them how they were enjoying the pizza! I told them that many of them were Sister's favorites; if they all stuck together and voted the same, she could not possibly take it out on all of them.

I know that deep in her own soul Sister Eileen was merely trying to teach me a valuable lesson. Just as with my father, her soul and mine were one. We were doing this dance together because, ultimately, what we learned would bring us closer to remembering why we are here on earth, to do the most good. I gave Sister a gift and she gave me one. She helped me have more compassion in my life for those who do not think like me but have the absolute right to walk their own path. The creative way in which she set up the election sparked my own creative juices. I did not come to these realizations until I was an adult, but on some level I knew back then that I was learning a lesson. I think I taught Sister something about her feelings, too.

On the soul level, she was the spirit of God. When her methods for teaching students like me made her angry and frustrated, she knew that she was separating from her true spirit because it didn't feel good. She knew on some level that the way her ego was operating wasn't kind. She must have known that teaching should be filled with joy and happiness. Going back to the convent at night, knowing she was butchering the feelings of a fourteen-year-old boy, must've felt awful. I felt no great joy either in butchering the feelings of the sister to teach her a lesson and make my point. Neither of us was operating within Spirit. It was a valuable lesson for both of us. Both egos were in full view during this whole operation. The ego wants to be right, control, and justify, and all those impulses were driving this very human interaction.

I had done all I could to keep my office. My future as president was now in the hands of the students. The day arrived for the vote and I gave my speech to the class, presenting my case. It was all quite formal and I was more embarrassed then nervous. I was also wondering how well the pizza party had worked. Sister Eileen stood up from behind her desk and announced to the class that the time had come for the impeachment vote. The vote was private so that I would not hold a grudge against those who voted against me. Her ego loomed larger than mine at that moment because she just knew to her core that I was going to be impeached.

I heard a sigh of relief from the pizza kids when she announced an anonymous vote. The sergeant at arms would tally the votes.

Sister very coldly told me to leave the room for the vote. "Yes, Sister, but where do I go since I'm not allowed in the hall alone?" I asked. She responded that if I was confronted, I should just knock on the door and she'd vouch for me. So I left my third-from-the-end last-row "you're not a good student" seat and started the long walk down the aisle like a dead man walking to his execution. The feeling of embarrassment I had giving my "please spare me" speech had given way to full-blown "I am not worthy" shame. Still, I held my head high and went out into the hall to be by myself—or so I thought.

As I stood by the door awaiting my fate, another bastion of kindness and mercy—Sister Confessor, the school's principal—approached on her hourly rounds of sniffing out sin. She had nabbed me in seventh grade and I'd been forever banned from being in the hall unchaperoned. Now she waddled down the hall as I stood in it without supervision. "What in God's name are you doing in the hall, Mr. Touhey?" she bellowed. When I told her, "Sister, I have permission from Sister Eileen so I wouldn't interfere with my impeachment hearing," she became very understanding!

That hadn't been the case the year before when I was in seventh grade. I'd asked Sister Alice Eddy if I could use the bathroom. Instead of using the bathroom, I went over to look into the glass window in the door of the eighth-grade classroom, where there was a

girl I liked. I was making faces to get her attention when I felt a tap
on my shoulder. It was Sister Confessor. She took me back to the
classroom and told Sister Alice Eddy I was never, under any circumstances, allowed to leave the classroom. I also had to go to confession with Father Delmonico to ask forgiveness for lying. I nearly wet
my pants about ten times over the next year while living under the
"Touhey lockdown."

Sister Confessor shared with me that it was probably best that I
wasn't class president, then continued down the hall on her way to
her other function at the school. She stood in the men's room on the
scheduled pee break to make sure everyone hit the urinal properly.
Sister also distributed report cards to every grade level. It was always
a blast just waiting for the last row to be called up. We waited in
line to hear a pearl of wisdom from the principal. For me it was usually something like, "Mr. Touhey, you are such a disgrace; grades like
these, and you, the class president."

Finally the sergeant at arms came out and said, "Come on, Touhey,
the vote is over." He led me back into the classroom and stood in
front of the class to announce the result. I hadn't been impeached
after all! Sister Eileen proceeded to yell at the whole class, "You have
all made this a huge popularity contest and I am suspending all class
meetings until Mr. Touhey learns parliamentary procedure."

I never did learn and there was never another class meeting. I
served out my term as a lame duck. Though I kept my office, I felt no
joy, just relief. The tension, shame, and embarrassment had drained
me of the energy it takes to be happy. I was like many people who
spend so much energy striving for the end goal that reaching it is
anticlimactic and doesn't feel good.

I have healed my heart over these incidents. I often wondered
what feelings of resentment in Sister prompted her complete rejec-

tion of me; maybe she was jealous of my spirit and sense of freedom. She was a very creative, talented woman in restrictive costume, working in an equally restrictive vocation. She left the convent not long after I graduated. My trouble with nuns wasn't limited to Sister Eileen. Maybe my intensely free spirit was a strong reminder of how subservient and compliant with authority the nuns had to be.

The fact remains that I was at one school for four years and that stability was significant. I felt I was part of the Sacred Heart community. I was in class with the same kids for four years and saw the same teachers and priests. My brothers were in school with me and we walked to school each day with the other kids from the neighborhood. We were a big team of young kids. I blossomed in the security of being in a community. I had not experienced the feeling of belonging since I lived on Newark Avenue in Bloomfield, with all my relatives nearby. I was happy as I had not been in a long time.

Even though I didn't excel academically, I was developing the belief that I was a valuable person because of how I excelled in the social aspects of community. I had found a niche in which to operate and express myself. I felt appreciated by my peers for the vibrant enthusiasm I possessed. That niche served me well and it still does.

LESSON 10

ATTITUDE INSIGHT

An attitude is basically the way you think. Having a positive attitude will bring positive results. The opposite is also true: a negative attitude will bring negative results. By examining your thinking you can identify the attitudes that hold you back and change them. In addition, you can build on the attitudes that move you forward.

You have a choice on a daily basis to have a positive or negative attitude. We cannot change the way people act; what influence our past, parents, siblings, or friends have had on us; or what the weather is like. We *can* control the way we perceive these factors and what significance we give to them. It is virtually impossible for a person with a negative attitude to sustain success and happiness over a long period of time. Your attitude is like the director in life: you can only pretend to have a positive attitude for so long. The real you will eventually emerge.

Exercise 9

ATTITUDE ASSESSMENT

1. Please list three traits you have that reflect a positive attitude.

_____

_____

_____

_____

_____

2. Please list three traits you have that reflect a negative attitude.

_____

_____

_____

_____

_____

3. Does your attitude change given the situation?
Yes_____ No_____ If yes, describe how.

_____

_____

_____

_____

4. What is the negative attitude you would most like to change?

_____

_____

_____

_____

_____

5. What is the positive attitude you would most like to build on?

_____

_____

_____

_____

_____

Each day for the next two weeks, be aware of how the negative and positive attitudes you chose in questions 4 and 5 affect your daily thoughts and actions. Please use an index card for each day. Put the date on the top of the card and describe your experience each day.

WHAT'S YOUR STORY?

Please journal about your own attitude. What do you plan to change?

_____

_____

_____

_____

_____

_____

_____

_____

_____

_____

_____

_____

_____

_____

_____

_____

14

The Miracle of High-School Sports

"THE MOST POWERFUL WEAPON ON EARTH IS THE HUMAN SOUL ON FIRE."

— *Ferdinand Foch*

By the time I entered high school, basketball had become my favorite sport. I was much better in baseball, but I loved basketball. I made the freshman basketball team and I was thrilled. I felt I'd arrived socially as a result of it.

The importance of participating in competitive sports was about to reach a new level in my life. The summer of 1968 is when I arrived as a true top-notch basketball player. I knew I was not going to play baseball the next season, so basketball was what I pursued. I spent every day that summer playing basketball at Crescent Playground. I'd go down the hill to the court before anyone else and practice drills by myself before the official pick-up games began. I was truly inspired to be the best I could be.

In those moments by myself, I was in heaven. I set a goal to be a starter that upcoming season, which was my junior year. I was determined to be in the lineup next to my best friends, Mike and Danny; we called ourselves the "terrific trio." I was focused on that outcome, but also fully present in each moment as I trained to attain that ultimate goal. In the purity of those moments I challenged myself to enjoy the marrying of mind, body, and spirit. I was very creative and invented many ways to compete against myself. There was always a magical feeling present in those moments. For so many years as a youngster, I had invented make-believe games to keep myself occupied. Those made-up games were always so much fun. As a natural outgrowth of that training, I became the best basketball player I could possibly be.

> *It is very important that we set goals that are attainable. Goals can be set high, but they must be realistic. Goals are the individual, step-by-step process of making dreams come true.*

I learned a lot about myself in those moments of solitude. I arrived at an inescapable truth: I was able to tap into an uncommon source of inner strength. I was aware of a presence inside me that had tremendous fortitude. As I worked out, my spirit, will, and determination would not be dampened by the fact that Coach Luciano was in no way counting on me as a premier varsity player. I cannot blame him, since I hadn't even been a starter on the J.V. team the previous year. However, there were forces at work in the essence of my hope and optimism that could not be denied. I was not only setting a goal to be a starter. I know now that I had a spiritual intention to improve to the point that conditions or circumstances could not deny me that goal. I faced a flood of challenging conditions and circumstances over the next nine months that could have discouraged the most diligent athlete, but I would not be denied. The legacy of hope I had received from my parents before my birth and the spiritual message from Regina after her death would propel me through some difficult moments to come.

I wasn't a starter the first six games of my junior year. In January 1969, an amazing thing happened; no coincidence! My best friend, Danny Benz, became ill before our first conference game against Jefferson and I replaced him in the starting lineup. I was an unknown quantity for the last time. I never again left the starting lineup. In fact, I was the leading scorer in that game and for the rest of the season. When Danny came back to the starting lineup, Mike Harry went to the bench. So two and a half years after miraculously making the freshman team and one year after forcing my way into the varsity dressing room, I was in the varsity starting lineup at Dover High School. I was truly in heaven right here on earth.

DEFINING MOMENTS IN BASKETBALL: LOVE OF THE SPORT AND TOUHEY FAMILY HONOR

Much had happened over the preceding nine months. Many trying experiences came my way that could have caused me to quit, but I held onto my dream. I used the inspirational and heartfelt encouragement of my friends and my sister Maureen to keep going. My path to the Dover High School starting lineup was a series of everyday miracles.

As I've said before, all it takes is a true measure of self-awareness to know that miracles are surrounding us all the time. I pay attention to each and every circumstance in my life today. I realize, beyond a shadow of a doubt, that purposeful intentions, combined with divine inspiration, have always set the course for my life's events. The God or spirit within me, along with my most predominant thoughts and feelings, was always a key component in the course my life was taking. I just wasn't aware of it back then.

Rather than sleepwalking through life, wondering why certain things are happening, bring awareness to your own thinking and feeling states. The miracles that can happen for an optimistic person are truly amazing. When you live your life on purpose and with intention, you will be able to direct its course in a way you may not have thought possible.

I did not just set a goal to be a starter in my junior year. I set an intention to be a starter. I was not going to let the challenging circumstances of getting into the lineup stop me from the vision I had about running out onto the court when the starting lineup was announced.

It is crucial to set goals that challenge us, that keep us moving forward.

The summer before my junior year, Mr. George Wilson, the basketball coach at Mountain Lakes High School, opened a basketball camp in Honesdale, Pennsylvania called the Camp of the Lakers. One of the most important gifts that I derived from going to the Camp of the Lakers was getting to know all the players from teams we would play against during the school year. It reinforced my intuitive, deep-seated knowing that relationships with competitors need not be adversarial. Playing with these guys at camp and then against them in the winter made the experience of competition very rich for me.

The ever-present poverty that permeated all situations facing the Touhey family reared its ugly head in this circumstance too. My parents couldn't afford the cost of sending my brothers and me to this camp. They had an arrangement with Mr. Wilson that Brian and I would work in the kitchen and cafeteria to defray some of the cost and they would pay the rest. But they never paid. Like all the other bill collectors, Mr. Wilson had to call the house asking for the money.

I have a deep feeling of appreciation for Mr. Wilson. He knew I was truly sorry and embarrassed that my parents did not pay. He was always so nice to us and never treated us any differently than the kids who paid. He tacitly knew the Touhey boys needed to be part of this camp for much deeper reasons than playing basketball. He realized how important it was for us to be part of this whole camp adventure and that it was a wonderful experience for the struggling boys in our family. Brian and I cleared the tables in the cafeteria after everyone was finished eating. I didn't mind. I was grateful to trade kitchen labor for the opportunity to go to camp.

My daily practices that summer were about to bear fruit in the blazing August heat at the Camp of the Lakers. In the first two days of camp, it was evident that I wasn't the same player who had ended the season in March. My improvement was nothing short of dramatic, even miraculous. The miracle of my own optimism was becoming a practical reality.

It is important to note that I did set conscious goals to improve my game. Goals are important. They give us direction. But the most important factors in my dramatic improvement were the spiritual and passionate intentions I'd set to accomplish my goals. The combination of spiritual intention and right action is the breeding ground for miracles to occur.

It was important to me to make my dad happy, and that provided motivation. But I was attached to something much deeper. I was in touch with the complete joy I felt when I played basketball. I was carrying my father's expectations and they were a burden. But my undying spirit and love for everything that was part of this commitment to basketball was the real driving force.

The appreciation of the coaches did not go unnoticed, either! They thought they were recognizing a relentlessly hard-working, hustling player. "He gets the most out of his ability," they said. "He treats every drill, every play in the game as if it is his last."

What was really happening was twofold. Yes, I needed to be good because it was important to the family, especially my father. The pride he derived from athletic success was crucial to him. But more important was my absolute connection to the spirit of sports, that inner fire I had for competing. What drove me to get better every minute was a spiritual component: the love for my friends, Danny, Mike, and Dave, and my desire to be on the court with them when the game started. The three amigos dressed in orange and black, winning for dear old Dover High. I wanted to belong. The coaches witnessed the manifestation of my spiritual intention right before their eyes. I was not just setting a goal. I was adding powerful, heartfelt intention to the task at hand. I was not consciously aware I was doing this, but I felt it very deeply inside.

The first day of camp I played the best I had ever played. The second day I topped that. While I was cleaning up in the cafeteria after dinner, Coach Luciano came up to see me. He congratulated me on my play and encouraged me to keep up the good work. I assured him I would.

As he was ready to step away, he said that if I kept getting better, he was going to have a hard time keeping me out of the starting lineup! I was on Cloud Nine. My confidence level soared. Each day I worked harder and played better than the day before. On the third day of camp, the coaches chose me to be Player of the Day. When camp ended and awards were given, I was chosen for the coaches' award, which signified hustle and improvement. I had my picture taken with the trophy. It was my first basketball trophy.

LESSON 11

GOAL-SETTING — PART ONE: IDENTIFYING AND ACHIEVING GOALS

It is very important that we set goals that are attainable. Goals can be high, but must be realistic. Goals are the individual step-by-step process of making our vision and life plan a reality. It is crucial to set goals that challenge us, that keep us moving forward. Sometimes people set goals that are too high for them to reach. This leads to a tremendous amount of frustration and, ultimately, failure.

A good way to experience success and strengthen the goal-setting muscle is to set some short-term goals. All of your goals should be based on your value system. When you set goals based on what is truly important to you, obstacles and problems that arise will not impede your progress. You will be more committed and persistent in your effort to reach your goals.

Many people pull up short of achieving their goals out of fear that they may fail. They give up too soon. It is important to use fear to propel rather than paralyze. Overcoming fear by staying committed, persistent, and consistent can give you the emotional intensity you need to support your goal attainment.

Creative goal-setting includes three important elements. They are the ability to set and monitor long-term or outcome goals, mid-term or performance goals, and short-term or task goals.

While setting goals, look at the end or outcome first and then work backwards. Performance goals are important for consistent measurement of whether or not you are giving yourself the maximum chance of achieving outcome goals.

Task goals are where champions live and breathe.

Exercise 10:

CREATIVE GOAL-SETTING

1. How do you react when you set a goal and you don't achieve it?

_____

_____

_____

_____

_____

2. Is it important to achieve every goal you set? Why or why not?

_____

_____

_____

_____

3. Practice creative goal-setting by writing one very important outcome goal that you hold for yourself.

_____

_____

_____

_____

4. List the mid-term or performance goals you will need to be sure you are on track.

_____

_____

_____

_____

_____

5. List the task goals you will need in the short term to be sure you are able to accomplish your performance goals.

_____

_____

_____

_____

_____

WHAT'S YOUR STORY?

Please journal about your own goals and aspirations. In relation to your goals, are you where you want to be in life? What do you plan to change?

_____

_____

_____

_____

_____

PART
5

PERSONAL GROWTH

In life we are either taking a step forward or taking a step backward every day. If we are able to look at all the conditions, circumstances, and situations as opportunities for personal growth, we are on our way to living the optimistic life of our dreams.

In fact, if we remain optimistic regardless of whether we think the circumstances, conditions, or situations are good or bad, we will experience tremendous growth.

We will be confident that we will handle all that comes our way as just an opportunity for us to acquaint ourselves with ourselves, as Emerson said. Nothing more, nothing less. An integration of mind, body, and spirit is possible from this particular perspective. When you are ready to change your perspective to one of optimism, your life will change to something beyond your wildest dreams.

15

The Miracle of College Basketball

"I FELT THAT I HAD THAT WINNER
MENTALITY INSTILLED IN ME."
— *Michael Jordan*

Because of my grades, I was unable to consider many colleges. I was not recruited by many schools, and it's a miracle that Coach Jack Martin recruited me to come to the County College of Morris. I would not have to pay anything to go to CCM. In the spring of my senior year, I went to a luncheon with my dad. At the luncheon, which included players from all over the state, I was awarded a scholarship to CCM for being named Most Promising Athlete in Morris County. I was very proud, because that was a great accomplishment. It was a financial award that would cover most of my costs. In addition, Mr. Joe Nazzaro, the financial-aid director, made sure that I received enough aid to cover the rest.

What I remember most about the luncheon was seeing my dad so happy. People from our past were there too, including Coach Joe Gravy and Coach Don Panhandle, who coached with my dad at Immaculate Conception High School and had coached my cousin Joe. My father's eyes were shining with pride as those coaches came over to our table to say hello and congratulate me. The miracle in this for me is the pure joy I felt in my heart. With my self-proclaimed purpose on earth to contribute to others and do the most good I could,

I felt more than just pride at that moment. My connection to these men went back to one of the most painful times for our family, the aftermath of Regina's death. These men represented our emotional and spiritual respite from the pain of her loss. They were also a reminder of my cousin Joe. We all were part of something together. With them, I experienced the intensity of the feeling of belonging to the larger whole.

Knowing that the depth of a feeling state is a matter of Spirit, the miracle for me is having had that spiritual awareness at all. I was aware that the sparkle in my father's eye went way beyond a conscious feeling of pride. It was the light of his soul shining through as a result of the connection we had with these men.

I have always possessed spiritual consciousness. My heart has always been open to seemingly small incidents and events. It is such a blessing. I feel the joy within me when I share stories with others about everyday interactions and occurrences and the miracles that are revealed in them. When you realize there are no coincidences in life, it adds a spiritual factor to EVERYTHING that happens. People often tell me that the level of detail I retain is amazing; what I find more amazing and miraculous is recalling the feelings in those situations.

> *A profound state of grace can be felt in your being when you pay attention to situations meriting gratitude in real time.*

Once again, sports provided the backdrop for some great human and spiritual interactions.

Life hadn't been kind to my dad since he last saw those two gentlemen. It was great to see him feeling so proud. The depth of what it meant to me and the feeling of joy in my soul were very special.

I entered CCM as a student athlete. My dad soon followed me there. He was out of work again, having lost yet another job. I approached Coach Martin, who was also the Athletic Director, to see if he had any jobs open. He said they were almost ready to create a new job as the athletic department equipment manager. I asked if my dad could come and talk with him about the job. Dad was hired and kept the job until his retirement. The miracle of competition and athletics provided my dad with a job he kept longer than any other he'd ever held. He sat on the bench for every home game I played at CCM.

Once again, my athletic career joined my father and me. I would go to work with my dad again. This time, I was paid for it, because it was my work-study job. I'd ridden on the milk truck, to the docks of Port Newark, to car dealerships, and now to the equipment room at CCM. I spent many hours in that equipment room chatting and carrying on with my dad. It was surely a spiritual experience and a blessing for us both.

I had a really good coach at CCM. Coach Martin was young, but he really knew the game. I found myself in a position similar to high school, where the coach slightly underestimated my playing ability. I had practiced really well as the first game approached. I was the sixth man on the team, the first player to come into the game off the bench. In preseason scrimmages I played very well. My father peeked in during practice once in a while. By now I didn't feel much pressure from him. I really bonded with him during the day when we spent time in the equipment room. But as the season progressed, things would change.

My buddies on the team were two guys I had competed against in high school, Ricky Testa from Morris Hills and Dave Osborne from Boonton. Dave had gone to the Camp of the Lakers. After college, Dave and I played in recreational basketball leagues for a number of years. I also befriended Pete Sacco. He was such a great guy, a good team leader. I played adult basketball with him after college. He played a key role in my one-year career at CCM. He was a steadying influence for me on the court, during games, and in practice. There were times when Coach Martin could be very difficult and demanding. Pete was a returning starter so he knew the ins and outs of Coach Martin's methods. Pete was 6'6" tall and played forward. We had two or three other players who were also that tall. I was 6'2", but I could play guard or forward. With a few days left before the game, it appeared I would not be a starter. I was lying on the couch at home one day after practice not looking too happy. My father asked if it looked like I was going to be a starter on opening night. I told him coach had not announced it yet. But I knew I wasn't starting (or was I)?

The next day in practice, Pete took a fall and hurt his elbow. He wasn't going to be able to play in the first game. There were bigger guys who were more natural choices to replace Pete in the starting lineup, but coach announced that I would be taking Pete's place. That was another miracle! Just as Danny's getting hurt made way for me in my junior year of high school, an injury played a major factor in my getting to play my first college game. Unlike in high school, though, I didn't have to wait six or seven games to get into the lineup.

The first game was going to be very special. CCM had built a brand-new athletic facility. My first college game would also be the first game ever played in the gym. It was also special because the school was only a few miles from our house, so the whole family could easily get to the games. Just like high school, when given the chance, I made the most of my opportunity. I scored fourteen points and the local paper ran a nice article about the game. It was really great! My dad was happy. My youngest brothers, Tim, Pat, and Mike, were in attendance. They looked up to me in a special way. Dennis and Brian were playing basketball at the high school. Brian was a starter on the varsity team at Dover High School. All was good on the home front because of sports.

It was a special time for me. I was playing well and making headlines at CCM. I went to all of Brian's games. The fans at Dover High congratulated me on my play at CCM. It felt great to walk into the Dover gym and be one of the more recognized athletes in the area. I was a former All-Star with a younger brother on the team and a star in my own right at CCM. I did feel appreciated, more than I had in a long time. Tim, Pat, and Mike were very good players in the CYO league, so it was great going to their games, too. My father was especially happy with my success on the court because he could go to work with his head held high each day. He fully enjoyed being the father of the team's leading scorer. He also seemed to enjoy who I was as a person. He really liked to see how others reacted to me. I was well liked. He witnessed firsthand how popular I was with my peers. Even though I never did any schoolwork, the professors enjoyed me, too. They chatted with him about what a nice guy I was. They only wished that I'd work harder in the classroom.

I felt fully appreciated by the Dover community. People enjoyed talking to me at my brothers' games. Though I was proud and somewhat cocky about the star status of the Touhey boys, I was really nice to people and they were nice to me. I was always talking to someone. My father often asked, "Are you running for mayor or something?"

I really felt like I belonged to three communities I loved: the Touhey family, the Dover family, and the CCM family. The spiritual juice that came from belonging and being included in those three communities cannot be described in words. The feeling was priceless. I felt surrounded by good. My needs for these two essential elements of appreciation and feeling included in something bigger than myself were being met in a big way.

It is no wonder that my emotional memories of this time in my life are so overwhelmingly positive.

Additionally, there was a little more consistency in my life. My father was still angry and moody at home. But I had a consistent and routine pattern of living that I had not experienced in a while. My father had a job. My mom and Kathy were working. We had sports. It seemed that there was more of a rhythm to life during that one year I spent at CCM.

DEFINING MOMENTS AT CCM

In January 1971, we were preparing to play our rematch game with Essex County College. The three days of preparation for the game and the night of the game became the defining moments of my college playing career.

Coach Martin came to me in practice and asked, "How would you like to cover Aron Stewart when we play Essex later this week?" Aron Stewart was their star player. He was the third leading scorer in the entire nation. I responded, "I would love to have a shot at him, Coach." Coach then said, "We are thinking of alternating you and someone else on him so you don't get tired chasing him around." I assured him he didn't have to worry about me getting tired. Since I was the team's leading scorer, he didn't want my covering the nation's third leading scorer to affect my offensive output. I knew he didn't have to worry about that!

One month earlier I had sat on the bench with my whole family looking on when we played Essex the first time. This time my father alerted my cousin Joey that he was not going to want to miss this game. I truly believe that this game, this night, was the culmination of my entire playing career. I had practiced all week on playing the dominant role in our game plan to contain Mr. Stewart.

Coach Martin devised a plan in which I would cover Stewart man to man, Ricky Testa would cover their point guard, and the rest of the team would play in a zone defense, so they were all just covering an area of the playing floor. All week at practice Coach had different people on the team pretend they were Stewart, and I chased them all over the court. He primarily used big players since Aron Stewart was 6'6" and weighed about 215 pounds. I was 6'2" and weighed 175.

In practice early in the week he'd asked, "Touhey, are you sure you will be able to handle this?" After a few practices he stopped asking. We both knew I could handle it, and my glances back at Coach had all the answer he needed.

This one game was a microcosm of every single thing that sports represented in my life. The preparation for this game and my participation in it were the culmination of all the positive life lessons I had learned through the medium of sport. There would not be another night like it, including the games that followed this one when I broke the school's scoring records. This was the night, and there never needed to be another game to define the person I had become.

As Shakespeare wrote, "All the world's a stage, and all the men and women merely players; they have their exits and their entrances; and one man in his time plays many parts." Well, the stage was set, all the players were present, and they all knew how to play their roles to perfection.

The major people in my life past and present were at the game. The key figures in the administration were in the stands that night. Many of them were sitting in the first row of the bleachers. The Dean of Students, Mr. Dragon; my history teacher, Mel Goldman; the director of financial aid, Joe Nazzaro, and many more. Each of them had helped me in so many ways to become a better person. During the school year they had expressed concern for me and spoken to me about my potential as a student and a person. Mr. Nazzaro always showed my family such care and concern. Mr. Goldman loved my father. I really loved that he saw through all my father's defenses and just loved him for the person that was underneath all the bluster.

I know that Tim, Pat, and Mike were there. I am not sure about Dennis or Brian. My sisters Eileen and Kathy were there. My brother-in-law Chick was there. Of course, my mom was there too. As I walked up the steps from the locker room, I thought about how special this night was. As I stepped out onto the court, I glanced across the gym. The bleachers were full. Another cadre of support, there to cheer us on, was the "bleacher bums." They were mostly returning Vietnam vets who would hoot and holler throughout the game.

The feeling in the gym was electric. In the pregame warm-up lines, as I ran by the bleachers, I saw the people who cared most about me in the whole world just cheering in delight. As I ran by them I thought, "Just wait until you all see, wait and see what I have in store for you tonight." The energy I felt was explosive.

> *Feeling appreciation for events as they are unfolding allows a mind-body-spirit connection. The feelings that follow provide the basis for being confident, alert, and totally focused.*

My cousin Joe was there. He had seen me play many times that year and I'd played some great games while he watched. But this was different. As I glanced up at him in warm-ups, time stood still for a moment. I could see myself as a five-year-old with him behind the backstop pleading with me to swing the bat. I envisioned myself as an eleven-year-old, the year Regina died, and the significance of being involved with Joey as he became a three-sport star at Immaculate High School. I felt what it was like to have my chest swell with pride at my cousin's athletic prowess.

With the sound of the cheering vets a muted background noise, I saw myself as a junior in high school in 1968 getting on the bus to travel from Dover to Joe's mom's house to record audio messages for him while he served in Nam. I'd leave basketball practice and travel one hour on the Lakeland line to Aunt Mary's house in Bloomfield. My father's sisters, Bridget and Margaret, Uncle Ed, and Joe's father, Clemont, were all there. We all told Joe how we were doing. Of course, I told all about my sports exploits. Aunt Margaret would say a word or two, and then she cried and could not continue.

My cousin Joe, the most important sports figure in my life other than my father, was in the bleachers now. His eyes were on me with the same love and admiration as mine had held for him eight years earlier when he competed. Only my father knew about the game plan, so Joe did not have any idea that his young cousin Kevin was about to accept the greatest challenge of his playing career by covering Aron Stewart.

My father, the equipment manager, was sitting on the end of the team bench as he had done for every game that season. I felt no pressure from him at all. This felt just like the time I had played for first place back in the Roxbury Little League and he stood down the third-base line shouting encouragement. I felt no pressure. I was totally in the zone.

The game itself was a thing of magic. I stuck to Aron like an additional appendage. There were times during the game when I glanced at the stands as I followed Stewart all over the court and saw everyone cheering me on to hold him down. His scoring average was thirty-five points coming into the game. I held him to fourteen points. Plus, I was the leading scorer in the game for us. I even scored the winning basket! We were down by a point with less than two minutes to play when Ricky Testa stole the ball. I saw him out of the corner of my eye and raced upcourt. Ricky threw me a perfect pass and I scored a layup to put us up by one point. Aron missed a shot with me in his face contesting it. I got the ball and was fouled, then scored consecutive foul shots to seal the win.

Aron Stewart hugged me after the game and told me I was a warrior, which was a real classy move. My cousin hugged me, my family congratulated me, and Joe came to the house after the game and the whole family talked about it for hours.

The best part was when I went down to the locker room as my dad was opening the door. First he shook my hand and then he gave me a bear hug. The look on his face was one of true appreciation, not just happiness for a job well done. He was saying thanks for giving our family this joyful respite from all the suffering and pain. It's no coincidence that the connection to his past, with his favorite nephew, Joe, added to the joy.

All the good that playing sports gave me was wrapped up in this game. My feeling of accomplishment went way beyond shutting down Aron Stewart. I experience that feeling whenever I even think about that night. I took in every feeling and sensation like it was the last time I would ever feel that way. I felt appreciated by everyone there. Even more important, I truly appreciated myself. I was part of a larger whole. By having me cover Stewart, the coach was telling me the whole team trusted me. And there was more consistency on the court that night than I'd had in my life in a long time. Everyone present—teachers, administrators, relatives, and my family—were contributing to my personal growth. They came from different parts of my life and they all cared about me for different reasons. All of these people were brought together by the saving grace of the Touhey family: a sports event.

> *To know we are included brings with it a powerful energy. To be part of a vibrant community where you feel appreciated provides a powerful, dynamic, positive energy. That is an awesome state of being in which to flourish.*

I went on to receive other accolades in my playing and coaching career. But the defining moment of my career in athletics was this night, this moment, and this game. My feelings and memories are so strong because the four essential elements all humans need to grow in a healthy way were present that night, right inside the gym at the County College of Morris.

Being grateful for all that happens, not just the good things, leads to appreciation. That feeling of appreciation is part of me in this story. Today I know that I had a taste of what it was like to have the four essential elements of development cooking simultaneously.

Though I was just a freshman only three-fourths of the way through my first year in college, my playing career would be over in less than a year. But I thank God every day for that peak experience in January 1971, the night I shut down Aron Stewart and received a very large dose of Appreciation, Inclusion, Consistency, and Personal Growth.

Maybe things were just too settled to satisfy my father. Too much consistency. The "waiting for the other shoe to drop" was a condition familiar to the entire Touhey family, and it was about to come into play.

My dad thought I'd better get out of Dodge while the getting was good. While sitting in his office one day basking in the good that had just happened during the basketball season, my father said to me, "You know, maybe you should consider looking into transferring to a four-year school now." I had had a hunch about this during the season when my cousin Joe made contact with Providence College about me. They came to a game where I did not play my best. I think the scout told Joe, "He couldn't play at a good grammar school." I was happy with the assessment because I wanted to stay at CCM.

My father remembered that Tennessee Wesleyan had been interested in me when I was in high school. Mr. Wilson had gone to school there and knew the basketball coach very well. At the time, the process of me contacting Mr. Wilson, the Tennessee Wesleyan College coach contacting me, and me getting on a plane to go down for an official visit seemed to take on a life of its own. Today, I know I was making a choice. Though I knew even then that this wasn't a good move for me, I pretended it was. The rest, as they say, is history.

LESSON 12

GRATITUDE, AWE, AND INTENTIONAL STILLNESS

"GRATITUDE IS AN ALL-OUT EXPERIENCE.
IT'S CHEATING TO BE GRATEFUL ONLY
FOR THE GOOD THINGS THAT HAPPEN
AND TO SHUN THE BAD."

— *M.J. Ryan*

As Margaret Stortz wrote in the October 2006 issue of *Science of Mind* magazine, "Living an actual spiritual life in today's world really demands consistent spiritual practices, growing ourselves up at any age, every day." I do not mean religious practices. I believe spiritual practices start with one thing: STILLNESS.

In stillness, the ego is quieted. In stillness, present awareness can be found and the fast-paced world filled with negative messages can be checked. "The madness is caused by thinking without awareness, which is how the ego keeps us in its grip," said Eckhart Tolle.

In stillness, you can become curious. You can awaken the spirit. You can use an intentional state of appreciation to become awe-struck by all those things in your daily existence that are supposedly insignificant.

In stillness, you can feel the awe of being part of one magnificent whole. Being in awe satisfies the human need to feel part of something. To know we are included in a community of powerful, dynamic, positive energy is awesome. Being in awe is a very optimistic manner in which to live. In the book *A Private History of Awe*, Scott Russell Sanders writes, "The experience of awe requires humility." In stillness, you can become awestruck. The ego cannot stand the light of intentional gratitude and appreciation. In the quiet solitude of a human spirit basking in the light of heartfelt awe, ego doesn't exist. Sanders continues, "Expect miracles, intend to receive, and be part of miraculous occurrences."

LESSON 13

THE MIRACLE OF STILLNESS: RITUALS THAT COMPOUND AND RADIATE THE FEELING STATE OF GRATITUDE

It is in stillness that you can begin to get centered enough to engage in what I call practical appreciation or gratitude. The absolute key to compounding the feeling of appreciation is to ritualize the feeling state of appreciation on a daily basis. The benefits are astounding.

Ritual is a crucial aspect of transformation. Ritual essentially *is* practice. Confucius saw ritual as the training ground that helps us empathetically deal with other human beings. Feeling and listening to others with empathy can be a precursor to true appreciation and gratitude.

In the June 2006 *Science of Mind* magazine, Lisa Hepner talks about stillness this way: "There is something inside of you that remains no matter what is going on externally." I believe, as Lisa Hepner believes, that when you become still you know "that is your place of happiness, your essence of joy, and your center of peace." It is from this heart center that the feeling state of appreciation and gratitude radiates.

It is a scientific fact that if you focus your attention on the area around your heart while breathing and feeling appreciation, a very strong "feelgood" hormone called DHEA is released into your system. The Institute of HeartMath has done exhaustive research in this area. The Institute's studies have also shown that the neural circuits in the brain can be altered, with positive results, by activating a feeling of appreciation in the heart. By ritualizing the practice of stillness and activating appreciation, you will condition your heart to the feeling. You can then call on the heart in your day-to-day living by just breathing and reminding yourself to appreciate, especially when the thousand interruptions of your perfect life come at you from all directions.

In her book *5 Gifts for an Abundant Life,* Diane Harmony writes, "When we are truly expressing appreciation for someone or something, there is a feeling that radiates from us that has its origins in our heart. The phrase 'heartfelt thanks' best describes the energy associated with authentic acts of gratitude and growing out of appreciation brings even more gifts." This is compound appreciation. It creates a very positive energy field all around us and others in our presence.

We may have been trained to think that having negative feelings is just a normal way of living. But while it may be *normal* in this day and age to feel negative about everything going on in our lives, feelings of gratitude and appreciation are a more *natural* state of being. When your system is aligned as a result of activating appreciation and a state of gratitude, the well-being of mind, body, and spirit is profoundly enhanced. You will not experience joy, peace, harmony, and abundance from a negative feeling state. It may be normal in today's world to feel negative, but it is not natural.

So it becomes a matter of choice. Harmony continues, "The simple truth is that one cannot at one and the same time experience appreciation and a negative feeling." The Institute of HeartMath research shows that the "stress hormone" cortisol is released from the same glands as the "feelgood" hormone DHEA. It is incumbent upon you to be responsible for how you want to feel. Feeling good is simply a matter of choice.

Exercise 11

GRATITUDE—GOING DEEPER

1. Please list at least five circumstances, past or present, that you think you COULD NOT POSSIBLY feel gratitude about. Describe in detail.

a. _____

_____

b. _____

_____

c. _____

_____

d. _____

_____

e. _____

_____

2. Please list at least five circumstances, past or present, for which you feel VERY, VERY grateful.

a. _____

_____

b. _____

_____

c. _____

_____

d. _____

_____

e. _____

_____

3. Please pick the most profound incident that you are VERY, VERY grateful for and follow these steps.

   a. Find a quiet place where you will be uninterrupted for half an hour.

   b. Be absolutely still. Quiet your mind. Sweep out all the thoughts of the day. You can use some soft music here if you wish. But being still in mind, body, and spirit is essential.

   c. Focus on the area around your heart. As you focus on this area, pay close attention to your breathing. You can see your breath as a beautiful color or you can count your breaths.

   d. Continue breathing this way for a while until you feel you have your system in such a quiet, still place that you are ready to bring that one profound incident of gratitude to your heart.

   e. From this pure state of stillness, feel the gratitude deep in your heart. Visualize your breath driving this feeling deeper into your heart.

   f. When you know you are in this elevated feeling state of complete gratitude, just be in it and feel it for as long as you wish.

   g. Gently bring your focus back to your breathing and the area of your heart if you find your mind wandering.

4. Each day for five days, after you complete your gratitude exercise, please do the following exercise. Take one of the incidents from your "COULD NOT POSSIBLY be grateful for" list and write about how you are looking at it from a state of gratitude.

WHAT'S YOUR STORY?

Journal about the change in your perspective below.

_____

_____

_____

16

The Miracle of Failing

"I HAVE MANY MEMORIES, AND IF I AM NOT
SURE YET WHAT ALL OF THEM MEAN, I AM
NONETHELESS CERTAIN THAT WHOEVER I
AM MY MEMORIES HAVE MADE ME; THAT I
AM BECOMING WHATEVER I CAN FIND OUT
ABOUT MYSELF."

— John Keats

In December 1972, a week into Christmas break, I was resting in my bedroom when my father kicked the door open. "Okay," he said, "you can quit school. Get your butt up to the county college and register for the spring term."

My first feeling was intense relief. That first semester at Tennessee Wesleyan had been a disaster, and on my return home I had broken the terrible news to my father that I did not want to continue there. Still, the look of anger, disappointment, and fear on my father's face as he told me his decision was hard to endure. I now understood that in my father's eyes, I was a failure.

Just a year earlier, life had been good in the Touhey household. I was traveling on the team bus with the County College of Morris basketball team. This was my first overnight trip as a college basketball player. In my possession was a plaque for making the tournament team in the Corning Christmas Tournament. My brother Brian was only a sophomore but already one of the best players in Morris County. He played at Dover High School and they had just beaten Morristown High School, a huge rival for Dover in those days.

My father's addiction to athletic success was being fed in an unprecedented manner. The six Touhey boys were all having tremendous success in 1970. I was a star at CCM, where my father was employed. Brian had a good football season even though he got hurt. Dennis had a great year in freshman football. The younger boys were all playing in the midget football program. Brian and I carried the fall success into winter and the family got its fix. Life was good—but fragile.

My decision to quit shattered the tenuous peace in the Touhey household. My relief at my father's pronouncement that I could quit was followed very quickly by a feeling of shame. By quitting Tennessee Wesleyan, I would be forfeiting a full basketball scholarship. The self-image that I had built, made up of MVP trophies, all-conference awards, and scoring records, would no longer exist.

Know that it is vitally important to bring the vision into the present. This is done by feeling what it will be like to realize that future as if it already exists.

Then there was my father's disappointment—my collegiate basketball career had just disintegrated before his very eyes. On top of my shame, I felt a terrible sense of panic, an awful "what now?" feeling. My self-worth had been fully invested in my ability to shoot an orange ball into a round ring with a nylon net hanging from it. If I could no longer do that, I was lost.

My father had been bragging all fall, to everyone who would listen, about my exploits in Tennessee. And now I was throwing all of this away. Not only did my identity depend on a successful athletic career—my father's identity and the family's pride rested entirely on the athletic success of us boys. As my sports star was waning, Brian's star was rising, both in sports and within the family.

To endure my feelings of shame and loss, I ended up drinking and partying hard. I blamed the coach at Tennessee Wesleyan for forcing me to quit. I desperately needed appreciation, a feeling of belonging, and some consistency in my life. Without the anchor of athletics, my life drifted, rudderless, with no feeling of hope.

Although I was proud of Brian, I felt ashamed that I had thrown away my athletic career. One night as I stood in the CCM gym and watched my single-season scoring record broken, I was sure the announcer would mention that the previous record holder was present! He didn't.

Quitting Tennessee Wesleyan should not have been the end of the world. I was only twenty years old. I had two more years of playing eligibility. But somehow I knew I was done. And I knew that I could no longer use basketball as a way to get appreciation, inclusion, and consistency in my life.

> *It is necessary to eliminate thoughts and feelings about your past limitations or present life circumstances that block you from getting a clear vision of the future. Keep your ego in check.*

In 1972, I met a young coed at CCM. Alice became the second girlfriend I had ever really had in my life. Through this relationship, I began to find those four elements that I so desperately needed. I began to feel *appreciated* for who I was as a person, not an athlete (she did not even know I was a former basketball star). She also provided much more *consistency* in my life. She and her family lived a quiet, stable life. She had six younger brothers. I felt I was a part of the family because they were all active in sports. I went to their games and played ball with them.

By July 1973, three years after graduating high school, I was married. I am sure that I loved Alice, but there was no way I was ready to undertake the responsibility of a marriage. I don't think I knew what real love was at this time in my life. I knew it felt like appreciation, inclusion, and consistency. I was optimistic that this was a new beginning for me. It felt like a miracle. I had found what I longed for. But there were difficulties. My peers were all entering their senior year in college. They belonged to fraternities. They went to keg parties. While they were having a ball, I was working forty hours a week and taking eighteen credits a semester so I could get married and graduate.

> *A vision is not a goal. A goal is something you achieve. A vision is something you can see and feel occurring without doubt or fear. In visioning, it is important to exist in a state of absolute optimism about what is possible in your life.*

A few days before the wedding, my father's anger and disappointment boiled over. I don't know what caused the outburst, but suddenly he was hollering at me from downstairs. "Why are you doing this? Why not wait a little while?" Of course, he was right. I don't know why he didn't bring this up when I first told him I was getting married. He must have held his feelings inside until they boiled over that night. Perhaps he finally realized that he was losing his eldest son way too soon to marriage.

As he came up the stairs after me, his rage continued to rise. "You are an idiot," he shouted. "What did you do—get her knocked up?" I had a quick flash back to an earlier time in my life when he beat me up. I felt scared as he took each step. The look of rage on his face was one I knew all too well.

I asked him, "What's your problem, Dad? You should be happy for me!"

As he reached the top of the stairs he grabbed me, slapping and punching me in the face. I did not retaliate, even though I could have. I did cry out for help. But just like that other time, my cries for help went unanswered. I backed away and pushed open the door where my sister Maureen and her husband, Glen, were sleeping. They sat up and watched with horror.

As I yelled—"Dad why are you doing this? Stop, please stop"— help came from an unlikely place.

My brother Brian was sleeping in the attic when he heard me calling out. He woke up and ran down the steps. He actually confronted my father!

"Dad," he cried, "don't you remember who this son of yours is? He has always been at your side, stood up for you, helped you and loved you. Dad, this is your oldest son, Kevin, the most loyal person to the Touhey family I know."

What courage Brian showed that night! The fight ended, I finished packing, and a few days later I was married.

LESSON 14

THE VISION OF YOUR LIFE

Most people think that having a vision is about the future. However, to truly make your vision powerful, it is important to bring the feeling state you desire for it into the present. Present-day life planning is much more focused when it is a natural extension of our vision of the future. This is especially true when you are able to access the feeling state that the future can provide, right here, right now. Let your vision fly; do not block its path with limitations based on past experience.

When you have a clear vision for your career path, relationships, family, and community, it is easier to develop a day-to-day life plan. It is important to step "out of the box" of your present circumstance when envisioning your future. Visioning is about creating a new, fresh reality.

Resist the very human, ego-based urge to "keep it real" while visioning. Even though vision seems not entirely logical at times, go for it anyway. The sky and beyond is the limit. You do not need to fixate on one single vision. Play with it and have fun. Your vision and life plan will evolve and become an absolute reality if you live in the present moment.

Goals are the individual step-by-step process of making your vision a reality. Goals are the process of laying out a plan of right actions that are aligned with your values and vision. It is crucial to set value-based goals that challenge you, that keep you moving forward.

The energy that comes from staying true to your values and vision will propel you forward toward complete satisfaction when you arrive at your goal destinations. Goals are the means you use to take the incremental steps to reach achievable targets.

If you set goals that do not reflect your values, it can lead to a tremendous amount of frustration and, ultimately, failure. It is important to monitor how you are feeling as you move along the continuum of goal accomplishment. This is why it is important to set some short-term and mid-range goals. You will be able to determine if you are on the right track toward making your vision a reality.

All of your goals should be based on your value system. When you set goals based on what is truly important to you, obstacles and problems that arise will not impede your progress. You will be more committed and persistent in your effort to reach your goals. Many people pull up short of achieving their goals out of fear that they may fail. They give up too soon. It is important to use fear to propel rather than paralyze.

Overcoming fear by staying committed, persistent, and consistent can provide the emotional integration you need to achieve your goals.

Exercise 12

ESTABLISHING A POWERFUL VISION

1. What is next for you in your life? Looking toward the future, what do you see for yourself?

_____

_____

_____

_____

_____

2. How does it feel to know you will make that vision a practical reality?

_____

_____

_____

_____

_____

3. Would you say that most of the conversations you have are about the past, the present, or the future?

_____

_____

_____

_____

4. What three things from your past or present block you from seeing your vision clearly? What do you need to do to eliminate them so you can start with a clean slate?

_____

_____

_____

_____

5. What is missing from life now that you want to include in your vision of the future?

_____

_____

_____

_____

_____

WHAT'S YOUR STORY?

Write your vision of your life. Be bold! GO FOR IT!!

    Now sit in stillness and imagine and feel what it would be like to have the vision of your life unfold just the way you want it.

_____

_____

_____

_____

_____

_____

_____

_____

_____

17

The Miracle of Forgiveness

> "FORGIVENESS IS THE GREATEST HEALER OF ALL."
>
> — *Gerald Jampolsky and Diane Cirincione*

I understand that forgiveness is no easy task. This is especially true of the most important aspect of true forgiveness, forgiveness of the self.

The ego screams loudly and clearly that we should focus on all the wrongdoers in our lives. I can assure you from personal experience that if you are able to hold up a mirror and be kind and forgiving to yourself, you are on the path to true freedom. As Leo Buscaglia wrote, "Forgiveness can never be realized in an atmosphere of accusation, condemnation, anger, and faultfinding." You will be unable to move forward on your path to true personal growth if you are full of blame and condemnation and engaged in default escape behaviors rather than dealing with issues you need to address.

"Forgiveness is not something we do for the sake of another person. Forgiveness is something we do for ourselves," says Greg Barrette. I could-n't agree more. The path to peace of mind and optimistic living has its foundation in forgiveness above all else. Caroline Myss wrote, "When we forgive somebody else, we are really forgiving ourselves."

Holding on to resentment is like taking poison and hoping the other person will die. It is always about you. Responsibility is about making a choice to feel more vibrant. It is your responsibility to move out of past hurts and into the true bliss of the present, without the excess baggage of condemnation. As David Augsburger puts it, "Forgiveness is letting what was, be gone; what will be, come; what is now, be." It is a freeing of self from the past and facing the future wiser, with renewed hope and faith. Forgiveness is often called an unconditional gift of love. This doesn't mean "I will forgive you if or when," but "I forgive you because I must if I ever hope to continue my own healing."

In a class sponsored by the Center for Conscious Living and facilitated by Reverend Pankaj Sharma, I was able to connect to the concept of self-forgiveness as never before. I learned that while forgiving all the people who had done me injustices (real or imagined), I also needed to forgive myself. By taking a hard look at the areas and actions of my life where I had served up an injustice or two, I got the opportunity to evaluate forgiveness in a new way. These were situations where my ego was in complete control. I am not suggesting you dredge up every little situation where you may have acted negatively in your judgment. Just be aware that it's very possible that by reacting from an ego state, you may have defaulted to behaviors that a new awareness would prohibit.

Pankaj Sharma shared a paragraph written by Catherine Ponder that speaks to the essence of this message: "Self-condemnation leads to dire results in matters of health and finances. Sometimes we are unforgiving of circumstances; an unhappy childhood, the loss or neglect of some material blessing. Sometimes we are unforgiving of God, blaming our losses, ill health and other problems on him."

I have lived most of the states of being that Ponder describes. Intellectually, I had already come to a measure of forgiveness for all those people who I perceived had victimized me in some way. In my process of psychological and spiritual growth, I laid the groundwork for a higher level of true forgiveness. This entailed letting go of judgments against any of the people, places, or things in my life that I thought had treated me unjustly. Even more powerful, I stopped my own ego from continually judging *myself* for all of the real or imagined injustices I'd committed. I stopped being the hypocritical bad guy in my own consciousness. When I really began to forgive myself, my actions and behaviors followed. When I realized that I was not exempt from wrongdoing and got real with myself, the level of forgiveness went to a depth that has brought with it peace and serenity.

DAD'S GIFT OF SILENCE

My ego left me in charge of a very special moment that I let slip away. That missed opportunity required self-forgiveness. It could have been a very healing moment with my father while he was on his deathbed.

This is a classic example of not being present in the moment. That is one of the most powerful dynamics of the ego: it will push you out of the present moment because all new experiences, learning, and changing occur in the now.

My dad was in the last days of his life on the physical plane. His bed with all he needed was set up in the family dining room and hospice was doing a wonderful job helping him make the transition. My sisters and brothers Kathleen, Eileen, Dennis, and Michael were with him around the clock.

> *Forgiveness begins and ends with you. When you really get down to it, forgiveness has nothing to do with anybody else, only yourself. There is a lot of power in taking this responsibility.*

On one of those last days, we were all at the house visiting him. He asked me to come and sit with him. He had one request; he wanted me to hold his hand and be silent with him. But I had already been drinking and was not at all receptive to the spiritual opportunity for healing that my father was offering.

In this moment, my father was entirely Spirit. The past no longer mattered. He wanted to leave me with the knowledge that he was truly sorry for any pain he had caused me. He wanted to give me the final gift of being connected as father and son. He was so enlightened in this moment. He just asked that we sit in this silent vigil of peace and healing.

Today I am in awe of the presence of God in my father as he died. He had a magnificent transition. In his last dying moment, he wanted me to know that he had always appreciated my recognition of the spirit inside his soul, regardless of how he treated me. He wanted to thank me for always loving him and to let me know that he respected the hope and optimism that my spirit provided for him. He appreciated the unconditional love I shared with him. He just didn't want to talk about it. His desire was that we simply sit in the moment and feel it together. There was nothing to be done. There were no more challenges or problems to be solved. There was just a father wanting to give a wonderful gift of silence to bond for the last time on the physical plane.

While writing this book I asked my brother, Brian, about how at peace he was with my father's death. I was so close to my father on the physical plane, while he and Brian hardly spoke in the years before his death. But Brian had a deeper spiritual understanding of my father's death than I did. I was grasping for a tangible last sign of forgiveness from him.

Brian described his last moments with my dad in a letter to me.

"I loved Dad very much by this time and realized that I was not going to be self-centered when I went to say my good-byes. I thought of all the effort he put into my life to help me be a success in sports; how deep down inside he really wanted me to succeed in the worst way; and how it must have been a hard break for him to see that dream not come true for him or me. As I sat there with him, I told him that now he could understand why I didn't succeed, that there were greater things I needed to do in recovery, and that I was very happy. I told him that I was happy for him that his pain was over and that he could see and understand why he was the way he was. I told him what a great pleasure it must be for him to see his Regina and

> *The key to forgiving and letting go resides in the present. Resist the temptation to go back into the past and make a list of all the people whom you need to forgive. It is imperative to let go of the ego's need to be right in order to forgive yourself or others.*

his grandfather's people who really loved him. I asked him to watch over me in a new and special way. Then I kissed him and closed his eyes and said good-bye." Alcohol and ego cost me my moment with Dad. I forced the issue of forgiveness according to my rules for healing, because after all, I was in recovery, not him. He was simply connected to God in the most profound way a human can be.

I kept asking him if he loved me. I pointed out a picture of him holding me on his lap when I was an infant. I asked him if he still loved me as he obviously had when the picture was taken. I persisted with questions and comments.

I remember how blue his eyes were, so vibrant and clear, as he gently asked me to just sit and hold his hand. But I was uncomfortable with the level of intimacy my father wanted. Extremely powerful forces of spirit were present. I got another beer, drank it, and pushed one more time for the affirmations my ego believed we needed—for him to apologize and for us to say good-bye to each other.

Eventually he became frustrated and called for my mother. He asked me to leave because he was tired. I kept drinking through the night, killing the pain of his impending death and my frustration at not being able to talk things out. I felt anxious over the discomfort I had made my father experience. So my ego jumped in to "save" me by letting me know that I was right to give my dad a chance to say he loved me before he passed over. For the next fifteen years, my ego justified my stance. Even on his deathbed my dad could not reach the level of intimacy he desired. Of course, I knew how he should do things. I was in charge of everything, including his death wish to show me how much he truly loved and appreciated me.

> *When you take full responsibility for forgiveness, you are able to recognize and embrace your own dark side. When you stop denying that shadow side, you can embrace the light, your spiritual birthright. This alone will help you forgive yourself for all past indiscretions.*

In the Foundations for Living class at the Center for Conscious Living, I became aware of this and began to explore the events from a perspective of spirit rather than ego. Now I am overwhelmed with love for my father and how he knew that we just needed to sit and pray in silence together and all would be healed. He knew this from his connection with his true and higher self.

Through both Foundations classes I have been able to forgive myself for not recognizing what he was trying to accomplish. That forgiveness has not come easily; I still feel a slight twinge as I write this. In my heart and in the silence of prayer, I have recreated those lost moments from 1989 and received the love that my father was trying to share with me that night. For the most part, I am content and at peace with the situation. I know that it just had to be that way so I could share my experience and contribute to greater self-awareness for others.

LESSON 15

FORGIVENESS

"No one can hurt you unless you think they can. For this reason all forgiveness is self-forgiveness."

— *Jon Mundy*

The purpose of this lesson is to help you realize that it is not just about forgiving others. To really get to a place in your life where you are not experiencing the pain that resides inside an unforgiving ego, you also need to forgive yourself. The desired outcome of this very simple exercise is for you to see firsthand that we truly begin to forgive others only when we look upon ourselves.

When you get in touch with your own wrongdoing, you will begin to forgive and see the perceived wrongdoers like us, neither better nor worse. We need to remember that we coexist as mortals in the world together, the wronged and the wrongdoer, and in our common humanity most situations can readily be reversed.

By taking an approach where I am compelled to work on being accountable for all my feelings, emotions, and behaviors and forgiving myself first and foremost, I have discovered the biggest gift of my lifetime. There is absolutely, positively nothing that is unforgivable in my life, nothing.

Charles Fillmore, the founder of the Unity movement, states:

"If you fear or if you are prejudiced against anyone, mentally ask forgiveness of it and send it thoughts of love. If you have accused anyone of injustice, if you have gossiped about anyone, withdraw your words by asking him in silence to forgive you. If you have had a falling out with friends or relatives, or engaged in contention with anyone, do everything in your power to end the separation. See all things and all persons as they really are— pure Spirit—and send them your strongest thoughts of love. Do not go to bed any night feeling that you have any enemy in the world."

> *When you learn the pathway to self-forgiveness, you can more readily see your own strengths and talents, as well as your imperfections. You become more willing to see the light in others and more willing to forgive perceived shortcomings.*

Exercise 13

THE ART OF ACTIVE FORGIVENESS: PART ONE

Forgiveness is freeing yourself from the past and facing the future wiser, with renewed hope and faith. Forgiveness is often called an unconditional gift of love. This doesn't imply "I will forgive you if or when," but "I will forgive you because I must, if I ever hope to continue to live fully."

1. Describe two situations in recent months when someone treated you in a way that you felt was unfair. Pick something that you truly have not forgiven the person(s) for yet.

_____

_____

_____

_____

_____

_____

_____

2. Describe two situations in recent months when you treated someone unfairly. Maybe you treated them with anger, as a failure, as if they were hopeless, or with frustration at their behavior, in such a way that you know they will have to go inside themselves to forgive you.

_____

_____

_____

_____

_____

_____

_____

LESSON 16

SELF-FORGIVENESS

"CALMNESS OF MIND IS ONE OF THE
BEAUTIFUL JEWELS OF WISDOM."

— *James Allen*

I believe that self-forgiveness is the key foundational concept to living a life filled with optimistic energy. It is imperative for you to go within in silence about this issue. The wisdom it takes to be in the state of grace with the concept of self-forgiveness is profound. You need to be gentle with yourself while exploring the ways in which you will need to forgive yourself.

In a state of calm, soulful reflection, you will be amazed to find that many of the things you need to forgive were self-inflicted. Your ego states of justification and self-righteous opinions will be the most painful to acknowledge and to forgive. The energy and freedom you will experience once you let go of all these negative feeling states about yourself will be a powerful experience, like nothing you've ever experienced until now. So let the "letting go" begin.

This is an all-inclusive prayer of forgiveness that I've used many times: "I forgive everything, everyone, every experience, and every memory of the past or present that needs forgiveness. I forgive positively everyone. I also forgive myself for past mistakes. God is love, and I am forgiven and governed by God's love alone. God's love is now adjusting my life. Realizing this, I abide in peace."

Exercise 14

THE ART OF ACTIVE FORGIVENESS: PART TWO

Sit in a safe, comfortable place. Close your eyes and take a few deep cleansing breaths.

Now visualize yourself in the feeling or situation you wish to forgive. See yourself in a place of true compassion and understanding as it relates to this incident. Be positive and affirm yourself in your heart. Say to yourself:

- I let go of self-anger.
- I now fully and freely release all negative thoughts about myself regarding this feeling of (fill in the blank).
- All that has happened is complete, now and forever.
- I free myself from self-condemnation.
- I feel the freedom in my soul that self-forgiveness brings with it.
- My soul has been craving this freedom. Forgiveness has liberated my soul!

Repeat this as often as you like. You now have the freedom to release all of the people and situations in your life that you have held hostage with an unforgiving heart.

WHAT'S YOUR STORY?

Tell a tale or two about your relationship to forgiveness.

_____

_____

_____

_____

_____

_____

_____

_____

_____

_____

_____

_____

_____

_____

_____

_____

_____

_____

18

The Miracle of Ease: Letting Go of Struggle

"YESTERDAY I DARED TO STRUGGLE. TODAY I DARE TO WIN."

— Bernadette Devlin

I used to believe that somehow I had to earn it if I was going to be blessed. I believed that at my core, I was a flawed person who needed to perform good deeds to be worthy. What I know now is something that I was unaware of for most of my life: What I believed in the present was setting the table for my future. So if my thoughts were primarily about all the ways I was flawed, I would draw to my circumstances the negative experiences that a person who thinks negatively draws to himself. My thoughts and feeling states in the present were drawing to me conditions that were positive or negative, depending on where I was focusing. I finally got it—I saw that I am totally responsible for drawing into my life all the things I am experiencing.

For instance, throughout this book I write about hope. I manifested and multiplied and radiated hope as a matter of spiritual intention. I had Regina to thank for reminding me of that with her visits to me.

It is important to note that I am very grateful for each and every thing that has occurred in my life. Whether conscious or unconscious, I drew those situations into my life so I could teach myself and others that we do not have to keep drawing negatives into our lives to learn life lessons.

If you keep recreating the past and keep the pain of it alive, you will draw into your life painful experiences to support that negative feeling state.

But you do not need or want to continue drawing pain and suffering into your life as the primary pathway to personal growth. My own predominant feeling state of authentic joy and optimism—in fact, all the good in my life—comes through ritualizing gratitude and appreciation for EVERYTHING and EVERYBODY.

All of the lessons and exercises in the book, wrapped around the stories I've chosen from my life, lead to the wisdom of this present moment. The past is gone. The future is a rumor. So now your blessed life's only focus is right here, right now.

The key to all these exercises is merely the awareness they bring to the present, moment by present moment. It truly is as simple as staying in the present and being in a continual state of gratitude. This is how the optimist inside all of us emerges. Life begins to become a blessed event when the miracles arrive one by one because the wisdom of optimism is now your filter. Now the manner in which you perceive the thousand interruptions in your perfect life is coming from a place of optimism. Those interruptions have no power in the eyes of an optimist.

I view all aspects of my life this way. Consequently, I am very wealthy. I have a wealth of loving friends, the wealth of two spiritually gifted children, and a wealth of exciting ways I contribute to the good of others. I am very wealthy with the love of my life, Annabelle.

Manifesting wealth of money, friends, life situations, relationships, houses, and anything else you desire is really just a matter of intention.

The purity of the feelings you bring to your rituals of intentions is the key. This is where optimism comes in. If you live your life with a pure feeling of optimism and develop this feeling through the bedrock states of appreciation and gratitude, miracles occur daily.

When you stay in the feeling state of gratitude by continually feeling not surprised, but awed, by the small and large miracles that occur, your optimism grows and grows. But make no mistake: it starts with appreciation and gratitude for EVERYTHING.

LESSON 17

THE MIRACLE OF MANIFESTING

The number one aspect of manifesting the life of your dreams is to feel good first. Many of the exercises in this book are geared to clearing out any negatives that may exist in your belief system, feelings, or thoughts. The vibrational signal you are sending out to the universe must be positive to let positives return to you. Start this process of manifesting the life you want to have by feeling good. It is a choice. Just do it!

The phrase "the sky's the limit" comes to mind. The most limiting question you can ask yourself while you are manifesting the life of your dreams is: HOW is this going to happen? Just leave that up to the Universe. If I had asked myself how I was going to write a book, have a family, live in this house, and raise my children, I would have been stopped in my tracks. Albert Einstein said, "Imagination is everything. It is the preview of life's coming attractions." I would add, be sure you are in a positive state of mind while imagining (visualizing) the life of your dreams. These aren't pipe dreams, they are real dreams.

Do not limit yourself in any way. You have the power to be and do as you desire. "What this power is, I cannot say. All I know is that it exists," said Alexander Graham Bell. So begin right now to see your future...and feel it. "All that we are is a result of what we have thought," the Buddha said. One of the messages from the movie *The Secret* puts it this way: "Decide what you want...believe you can have it, believe you deserve it, believe it's possible for you." The message continues, "Close your eyes and visualize having what you want already—and the feeling of having it." Be optimistic since that is when miracles arrive out of nothingness.

W. Clement Stone says it so well: "Whatever the mind can conceive, it can achieve." My life in the present is a living testimony to the truth of that statement. Nothing just happens to us, there are no coincidences, and everything that has ever happened and will happen has been manifested by us, through our thoughts and feeling states of being. PERIOD!!!

LESSON 18

MANIFESTING OUR HIGHEST GOAL

Goal-setting is a spiritual experience and exercise. It is a concrete way to see if you are integrating mind, body, and spirit. I learned the following goal-setting exercise in a class called Foundations for Living, facilitated by Reverend Dr. Carol Lawson, Reverend Jessica Bennett, and Practitioner Wade Bell. This helped me break through my last ego-based reasons for not finishing this book.

In week one of the class, Reverend Dr. Carol, founder of the Center for Conscious Living in Moorestown, New Jersey, told us to set goals we would like to have completed by the last class, week thirteen. In week two we were given an assignment to write an affirmation to support that goal. She then asked us to complete an exercise where we listed all the "yeah, buts"—all the things that we believed were stopping us from accomplishing the stated goal.

I wrote affirmations to support my goal of finishing the book. "Yeah, but," I said to myself as she was giving the assignment, I am soooo spiritually over having to write affirmations that I felt I was just going to waste the next two hours of the class. But I didn't want to act out like a fifth grader, so I began writing. I was in for a huge surprise. Reverend Dr. Carol's method put to rest any ego-based blocks that still existed.

So that you can try it yourself, I am going to include the exercise here.

First, Reverend Dr. Carol instructed us to write our affirmations. Mine was that my book, *The Miracle of Optimism,* was written, published, and sold. On the next line we were to write a "yeah, but." Then we were to write the affirmation again, and then another "yeah, but." These "yeah, but" statements followed each time I rewrote the affirmation:

- I do not have the time to sit and finish the book.
- How will I ever find an editor who won't laugh at what I have written?
- How will I find a publisher?
- Who on earth will buy it?

- No one will ever believe I was able to have any optimism after the way I was raised.
- My siblings will think I am full of crap.
- No one will believe the story of my sister, which is so central to the book's theme.
- There are a lot of books like this out there.
- Some of my friends will think I found God.

Then Reverend Dr. Carol instructed us to write more "yeah, buts" with our nondominant hand, and this is what followed:

- I am stupid. Almost every teacher said or implied that when I was growing up.
- I always got bad grades in writing and in English; how the hell am I going to write a book?
- They were wrong.
- I was wrong for believing them.
- I will be back to writing tomorrow.

Reverend Dr. Carol helped me renew the hope, belief, and knowing that I could finish writing this book, just with that one self-awareness exercise.

Exercise 15

THE "YEAH, BUT" EXERCISE

Please take fifteen minutes to become aware of any feelings, thoughts, or emotions you have that may be holding you back from living a fully optimistic life. Even the most minor ones are in the deepest level of your being, keeping you from having what you really want from your life. Be bold with your answers!

1. Write a goal for yourself.

_____

_____

_____

_____

2. Write an affirmation below supporting that goal. It can be about anything in your life you want to happen.

_____

_____

_____

_____

3. Now write a "yeah, but" statement after the affirmation.

_____

_____

_____

_____

4. Rewrite the affirmation several times, and each time write another "yeah, but."

_____

_____

_____

_____

5. After a number of "yeah, buts," write with your nondominant hand.

_____

_____

_____

_____

If done diligently, this exercise will help you start to uncover where your blocks to optimism are erected. Remember it takes energy to be optimistic and the "yeah, buts" are major energy drains.

"YOU CANNOT UNDERESTIMATE THE VALUE
OF A SIMPLE TOOL THAT IS USED EVERY DAY
OF YOUR LIFE."
—*Annabelle Estacio-Touhey*

The Last Exercise!!!

I leave you with a simple breathing exercise to feel in the depths of your soul what it will be like to manifest the life of your dreams. Feeling the satisfaction of having what you wish to experience in life before you actually manifest it will draw that experience to you with this simple yet powerful tool.

Have a happy, powerful life and know you are special in the eyes of God.

BREATHING IN GOAL SATISFACTION

1. Go back and find your goal statement, or bring another goal to mind.
2. Be aware of the affirmation you wrote to support that goal.
3. Close your eyes and breathe, focusing on the area around your heart. Just breathe for about a minute.
4. Keep your eyes closed and FEEL the power of your affirmation while you continue your breathing.
5. Go back to your goal while in this balanced state and FEEL what it is like to have accomplished your goal.
6. Imagine (mind) and feel (spirit) your goal as if it is accomplished!

There is no right or wrong way to do this. Just stay with it and practice for the next thirty days. Remember, it takes a ritual to change routine thinking and feeling states so you can establish new habits for optimistic living.

WHAT'S YOUR STORY?

Write about how, as a result of this book, you are going to start a new, more optimistic story about your life.

_____

_____

_____

_____

_____

_____

_____

_____

_____

_____

_____

_____

_____

_____

_____

_____

_____

Acknowledgements

It took a lifetime of experiences to write this book. It also took an amazing number of compassionate people who have loved and supported me over the years. These people all reside in a very special place in my heart. They have made such rich and valuable contributions in the formulation of all that was written on the preceding pages.

All my love to:

Annabelle Estacio-Touhey, my wife. There is no book without Annabelle. She has provided me with undying support during this project. Her devotion, love, support, and encouragement gave me the power I needed to write this book.

My loving daughters, Serena and Ava. You are both angels sent by God. Every day you help me connect with the spirit that resides inside all of humanity.

My parents, James and Hilda. My parents loved me. My mom has showed me that undying loyalty and perseverance produce results. My dad was my soul mate and greatest teacher. Although his methods were very challenging, he was the most dominant influence in my life.

My in-laws, Drs. Resty and Carmen Estacio. They have lived through the writing of this book at very close range. They have offered so much support, in so many ways, that there just would not be a book without them. Period.

Coach Frank Cagnosola, my freshman basketball coach. Coach Cag acknowledged the sacrifices I was making to improve my game. He kept me on the freshman team even though I was probably not good enough to make it.

Coach Pittas, my JV basketball coach. He was always good to the Touhey family. He probably understood better than anyone how much pressure my father put on us to succeed. He had a compassionate kindness about him.

Coach Patrick Luciano, my varsity basketball coach. His own dedication to making Dover High a force in high-school basketball inspired me to equal his efforts with my own efforts to get better. I know Coach cared about me.

Coach Jack Martin, my college coach. He helped the Touhey family survive by giving my father a job. He didn't fire him even though my dad should have been fired. Coach Martin recognized so completely my absolute love for the game of basketball. He knew I played with heart. My love for the game matched his love for the game.

Joseph Carter, my cousin Joey, my first sports hero. I just loved watching Joe play. I wanted to be just like him.

Robert Carter, my cousin Robby. I can see him jumping over the pile for a TD when he played for my dad in football. I used to love to watch him play hoops with Joe. I fell in love with basketball watching those pick-up games.

Danny Benz, my best friend. My boyhood partner, my lifetime friend, no matter what. We expressed our love for each other and the game of basketball by playing against anyone, anywhere, anyhow, anyway.

Dave Loeb, such a good friend. A gentle soul whose house I loved going to, just to hang out.

Michael Gruber, a steadying influence in my life. His kindness gave me the confidence I needed to know I was a worthy friend.

The Center for Conscious Living, where my family found a place to grow and know God in a powerful way. The founding Minister, Reverend Dr. Carol Lawson, has been an inspiration.

Ed Mickool, my first life coach, who helped me find my power as a human spirit.

Geoff Farnsworth, a gifted man who told me I was the definition of what a life coach should be.

CoachU. So many things I developed for my exercises and lessons, I learned from CoachU.

The Institute of HeartMath. I learned how to live in my heart in Boulder Creek, California.

The Girls of Will-Moor Gymnastics 2007. You were with me all the way on this project. We all lived the lessons of the book. Thanks to Emily, Briana, Kristy, Beate, Jordan, Amanda, Rebecca, Katie, Kirstie, Danielle, Darlene, and Kate.

Reverend Jessica Ayars-Bennett. Simply put, she is an angel.

Thank you to the thousands of students I have shared my story with over the last twenty-five years. You have been a part of this fantastic journey called "The Miracle of Optimism." I love you all.

CPSIA information can be obtained at www.ICGtesting.com
Printed in the USA
BVOW02s0636230315

392838BV00005B/7/P